Brain Science and Psychological Disorders
Therapy, Psychotropic Drugs, and the Brain

Brain Science and Psychological Disorders

Therapy, Psychotropic Drugs, and the Brain

F. Scott Kraly

W. W. Norton & Company
New York • London

For information about permission to reproduce selections from this book, write to
Permissions, W. W. Norton & Company, Inc., 500 Fifth Avenue, New York, NY
10110

Composition and book design by Paradigm Graphics
Manufacturing by R. R. Donnelley, Harrisonburg
Production Manager: Leeann Graham

Library of Congress Cataloging-in-Publication Data

Kraly, F. Scott
    Brain science and psychological disorders : therapy, psychotropic drugs, and
the brain / F. Scott Kraly.
        p. cm.
    Includes bibliographical references and index.
    ISBN 0-393-70465-3
        1. Neuropsychiatry. 2. Brain—Diseases. 3. Neuropsychology.
    4. Neurobehavioral disorders. 5. Human behavior. 6. Psychotropic drugs.
    7. Cognitive neuroscience. I. Title.

RC343.K925 2006
616.89—dc22

                                                                2005055476

W. W. Norton & Company, Inc., 500 Fifth Avenue, New York, N.Y. 10110
www.wwnorton.com
W. W. Norton & Company Ltd., Castle House, 75/76 Wells St., London W1T 3QT
1 2 3 4 5 6 7 8 9 0

To my dad, Fred A. Kraly (February 14, 1923–July 9, 2005).

Contents

Acknowledgments

Thank you to Anthony F. Aveni and Rebecca L. Shiner for advice and encouragement.

Preface

Let's say you don't know the answer to a question, and it does not seem possible that you could find the complete answer in your lifetime. What are you going to do when people demand that you teach them the answer to that question?

The question at hand is "What is going on in the brain of a person suffering a debilitating psychological disorder?" No one knows the complete answer to that question. In fact, we are in the middle of a continuing search for the answer—a search that employs powerful new research strategies and techniques that regularly reveal new facts with which to fuel today's contemporary wisdom regarding the answer. Today's contemporary wisdom is challenged as soon as the next day, however, as the largely uncharted frontier of the brain continues to be explored. That process of exploration gives us facts to support theories that are quite tentative. Given the tentative nature of our contemporary wisdom, I've taken the approach for this book that it is as important to understand the strategies used in the search for facts as it is to know some of the facts. Besides, you're more likely to remember how behavioral neuroscientists approach a question, how their strategies of experimental inquiry are both useful and limited, than you are likely to remember detailed facts about the brain.

This book covers four areas. For starters, it considers how disordered processes in the brain result in dysfunctional behaviors, and how different therapeutic strategies may target different aspects of psychopathology. Next, it gently introduces you to the structures and processes that contemporary neuroscientists think enable the brain to organize behavior and psychological processes, and it gives you some idea of how brain scientists conduct research to learn how the brain organizes behavior. Then it explores the contemporary wisdom about which processes in the brain are disordered when behaviors are dysfunctional. Finally, this book presents examples of how successful therapies alter processes in the brain when they improve behaviors. Composite case vignettes are used throughout to portray some clinical issues relevant to the topics at hand. In the end, what you'll find here are some facts and speculations and perspectives on how scientific investigations of brain and behavior can produce new facts that will facilitate the acceptance or rejection of some of those speculations. That perspective should help to prepare you for the continuing rapid evolution of our understanding of the relation between brain processes and behavior.

Now here's some advice for reading this book: Only an idiot would write a book with sections that were not arranged in the order that they should be read. However, there could be some benefit to reading Part IV prior to reading Parts I, II, and III. This short section is intended to provide an overall perspective of the vast terrain that is the field of brain science. That perspective certainly makes sense when read last, but it also makes some sense when read first—and it makes the most sense when read both first and last.

If this book is any good (whether read forward or backward), I need to thank the many students who have demanded, each and every semester, that I teach them as clearly as possible, as quickly as possible, using as few words as possible, while adding a little twisted humor to keep their attention. I hope this book holds your attention and that it is useful in some small way.

F. Scott Kraly
Hubbardsville, New York
August 15, 2005

Brain Science and Psychological Disorders
Therapy, Psychotropic Drugs, and the Brain

Introduction

> Meatballs. Mother and son had a heated argument regarding the meatballs on the morning of the Thanksgiving Day the adult son was visiting his mother in Brooklyn. The dispute ended with son strangling mother to death. No other details were provided in the newspaper's brief report—nothing about the character of their relationship, the son's medical history, or psychiatric diagnosis, nothing about failure to comply with taking his medication. The reader was left to imagine the explanation for the son's behavior on that Thanksgiving Day.

The behaviors of humans include the wonderful and the dysfunctional. Dysfunctional behaviors, exhibited by people who have disturbed emotions or thoughts, are generally viewed as having a rich, complex assortment of causes or explanations. And dysfunctional behaviors, like all other behaviors, have various immediate and long-term consequences.

One fact about dysfunctional behaviors—something well-known to mental health professionals—is quite revealing regarding causes: For almost any psychological disorder and its behavioral symptoms, a therapeutic alteration in the chemistry of the brain, nervous system, or physiology can produce a dramatic improvement. To put this point another way, just about any diagnosable psychological disorder has its chosen drug therapy among the assortment of therapeutic treatments for that disorder. This fact is so well known that, perhaps all too often, drug-induced alteration in the chemistry of brain is taken to be the preferred, convenient, quick-fix solution to dysfunctional behavior. So how is this revealing?

The fact that drug-induced alteration of brain chemistry can alter virtually any emotional or cognitive psychological process makes very clear that the chemistry of the brain is fundamentally involved in most or all of psychology and behavior. That does not mean that brain chemistry can explain all there is to know about behavior, but it does reveal that the brain presents a useful window through which to study dysfunctional behaviors and their underlying disturbed psychological processes.

So the remarkable clinical effectiveness of drug-induced improvement of dysfunctional behavior reveals that the chemistry of the brain is important for behavior, but where in the brain is this happening? Can we identify specific places in the brain or nervous system or physiology associated with specific emotional or cognitive problems? Can we identify specific chemicals in the brain that are associated with specific behavioral disorders? Can we understand how these brain chemicals are created and utilized and then become disturbed, leading to dysfunctional behaviors? And if we can understand each of these points, can we ultimately create drug and nondrug therapeutic interventions that act through these specific chemical processes in these specific places in the brain to improve symptoms of behavioral disorders?

Nicole is a member of a family with a history of depression. She has suffered the loss of a child in a tragedy, and she has a history of using alcohol to blunt some of the pain of her trauma. She overeats to cope and consequently has gained considerable weight, leading to diminished self-esteem. She has a spouse who is somewhat insensitive to her emotional needs. She is open to a plan to relieve her depression so long as the talk therapy is one-on-one, client and therapist alone, in the interests of protecting her privacy. These details from her life story reveal a complexity of past events and plans for the future, most of which may have contributed to the onset and maintenance of her depression, and also may have an impact on the likelihood of her recovery.

Can the entirety of Nicole's situation be understood merely by looking through the single aperture of brain chemistry? It does not seem likely. Even if a prescription antidepressant drug could alter brain chemistry in a way that led to the improvement of her symptoms, the drug therapy would not be directly effective for addressing a number of important issues in this woman's life. For example, giving Nicole an antidepressant drug will not make her husband more responsive to her emotional needs.

Although the study of the brain is a useful window for discovering processes that contribute to normal and abnormal behaviors, it is certainly not the only way we might look to improve our understanding of psychological processes and behavior. Consider this woman suffering from a debilitating depression.

Despite the facts that a drug-focused therapy will (1) not correct all difficulties faced by a patient, (2) is not likely to relieve all symptoms of a behavioral disorder, and (3) is not likely to "cure" a psychological disturbance, drugs are used as therapeutic devices with great success. So great is the success of pharmacotherapy for psychological disorders that it would be foolish not to at least consider pharmacological treatment as an option (just as it would be unwise not to consider nondrug options for treatment). And just as it might be foolish to reject drug-induced alterations in brain chemistry as a treatment option, it would be unwise not to understand how both drug and nondrug therapeutic options may alter the brain to relieve symptoms of behavioral disorders. The working assumption here is that drug therapy and perhaps many nondrug therapies alter brain processes to improve symptoms. And if you are in the business of using these therapeutic tools to help patients, you should also know something about how these tools work. A professional doesn't just use the tools of the trade; a professional knows *how* the tools work their magic.

The relation between processes in the brain and symptoms of psychological disorders is treated in four parts in this book. The chapters in Part I explore the relation between brain processes and dysfunctional behaviors, including the development of disorders, and the advantages and disadvantages of pharmacotherapeutic and psychotherapeutic treatment approaches.

Chapters in Part II introduce fundamental principles of brain organization and chemical processes that are related to normal and dysfunctional behaviors. Why do we need go to this somewhat technical level? First, it is clear from the clinical treatment of psychological and behavioral disorders that drug-induced alterations in brain chemistry are powerful and valuable tools for the improvement of psychological processes and behaviors. Second, it is clear from the wide variety of alterations in emotions, cognition, and behaviors that can be induced by drugs, that the brain and its chemistry are probably involved in all psychological processes and behaviors. Therefore, we cannot understand all there is to know about behavior or dysfunctional behavior without understanding fundamental principles about the organization and functioning of the brain.

My focus on the fundamental principles of brain organization and chemistry that are related to psychology and behavior will require a somewhat limited approach when it comes to details about structures and functions. Some simplification and generalization is necessary to make manageable a famously complicated topic. On the other hand, I will not insult you with the usual level of analysis presented on these topics in the typical undergraduate "introduction to psychology" class. Thus, I'm aiming for a middle ground that will serve two purposes: For one, it will help you see the great progress that has been made in understanding the relation between brain and behavior. It also will permit you to see some of the real limits of our understanding, providing a reality-based perspective that should be particularly useful for those who bear the responsibility of understanding and treating dysfunctional behaviors.

Specific behavioral disorders are covered in Part III. These disorders are examined with a focus on what is known and what is not known about the relation between symptoms and processes in the human brain, and what therapeutic approaches teach us about that relation. The concluding Part IV asks you to step back from some of the details to consider what we "really" know, and to get giddy and breathless about what the future may hold for understanding and treating dysfunctional brain processes and disordered behavior.

TREATMENT OF BEHAVIORAL AND BRAIN DISORDERS

Part I considers factors that contribute to the development of disordered brain processes and dysfunctional behaviors, how these contributing factors encourage the use of pharmacotherapy and psychotherapy to improve symptoms, and how successful pharmacotherapy can lead to hypotheses regarding which neurochemical processes in the brain are related to behavioral disorders.

How Do Disorders Develop?

> Hugs from Mommy were too few and far between to remember. And Dad was loving but largely absent, seeming to be "at work" all of the time. A few rejections by boyfriends seemed harmless enough. She was, after all, attractive, personable, bright, and a successful 38-year-old director of social services at a major hospital/health care complex. So the diagnosis of depression, accompanied by detection of urinary chemical markers indicating a tendency toward suicide, was somewhat surprising to friends and even to her.
>
> Which of these factors contributed to the onset of her depression? Was it the family social dynamics? Was it a hypersensitivity to rejection? Was it an inherited physiological defect or chemical deficiency in her brain that she had carried within her all these years? Or was it all of these factors converging at this point in her life that made her ill?

The causes of any of the various diagnosable psychiatric illnesses are difficult to identify definitively. Whereas it may be easy to enumerate potential sources of difficulty, proving that one or the other factor was a principal cause can be next to impossible, in large part because the patient and the therapist are looking back in time, wondering which of these factors brought the patient to where he or she is now.

Looking back at the patient's "life story" is useful in attempting to identify issues that may remain unresolved and which can now be addressed clinically. Looking at the "now" is also useful in identifying contributing factors (e.g., the stress related to dealing with a terminally ill parent), including any physiological abnormalities that may be related to behavioral symptoms. Knowing the patient's history *and* being familiar with the current situation are important for the immediate task of formulating a plan to help the patient.

We ask: *How* did this patient with depression get to where she now is? Can we boldly (perhaps foolishly) claim to have a broad theory that explains the development of all cognitive and emotional disturbances? Let's try this: A general model that may serve is a framework in which the likelihood of illness is determined by a combination or interaction of a specific inherited predisposition (a neurochemical vulnerability, perhaps) together with previous and current environmental or social stressors. Just as a person might inherit a tendency to develop high blood pressure that is exacerbated by poor dietary habits, weight gain, and a sedentary lifestyle, so too might a person inherit a tendency to become depressed. And when life's traumas begin to present themselves, symptoms of depression develop for that vulnerable individual.

Interaction of Vulnerability and Stressor Causes Illness

What is assumed to determine the onset of an illness (e.g., depression) is not the inherited neurochemical predisposition alone, and not only the stress of the dying loved one, but the combination of the inherited predisposition *and* the life crisis. Another individual, with an inherited predisposition for addiction, for example, may not become depressed but may develop alcoholism when faced with a similar life crisis. The salient feature of this model is the *interaction* of vulnerability and the stressor. Moreover, this model includes the possibility that specific (neurochemical) vulnerabilities in the brain and nervous system are likely to predict specific categories of illness, and that specific stressors may also predict specific categories of illness. For example, someone with an inherited dysfunctional norepinephrine neurochemistry in the brain may be more vulnerable to becoming clinically depressed, as 10 years of living with an oppressive spouse gradually becomes unbearable. In contrast, a person with an inherited dysfunctional serotonin neurochemistry in the brain may develop an anxiety disorder when faced with a similarly oppressive spouse. Absent these marital stressors, however, neither of these people with inherited vulnerabilities may become ill with a depressive or anxiety disorder.

Brain Processes May Establish Vulnerability for Specific Behavioral Dysfunctions

Neurochemical processes are incorporated into this model in the following way: The brain, nervous system, and peripheral physiology may well be the site(s) of inherited (or behaviorally induced) vulnerabilities. Some dysfunction in the brain's neurochemical processes may establish that person's underlying vulnerability to one or another specific psychiatric disturbance. Moreover, such a neurochemical disturbance in the brain may coexist with disturbances in the peripheral nervous system and in physiological processes—such as the deficient release of a hormone in the intestine during eating (predisposing one to bulimia)—and some of these various problems may be more likely to occur in one or the other gender.

How do these vulnerabilities in the brain, nervous system, and physiology come to be? First, a neurochemical vulnerability in the brain may be *inherited*. Evidence to support this notion includes the higher incidence of psychiatric illness (e.g., psychosis, depression, addiction) in descendents of families with a history of that illness, and higher incidence of concordant illness in pairs of monozygotic (i.e., genetically identical) twins raised in separate social environments. Second, a neurochemical vulnerability may be *created*: Examples include neurochemical changes in the brain induced by drug use (illicit or therapeutic), and those induced by chronic stress or brief trauma. The chapters in Part III consider specific neurochemical vulnerabilities for specific behavioral dysfunctions, including some that occur with greater frequency in one gender than the other.

How do we explain the fact that 25-year-old Jen is an alcoholic, but her 25-year-old roommate, Cheryl, is not? They both consume comparable amounts of alcohol in social settings. Neither young woman has a family history of alcoholism or addiction to other drugs. Jen and Cheryl grew up together, had similar life experiences, with the only notable difference being the fact that Jen infrequently experimented with alcohol and marijuana for a year or two early in their high school years. Jen's usage was not unusual, given the frequency of usage among her peers, and she did not seem to "have a problem" then. But did that early adolescent usage, though infrequent, induce in her a neurochemical vulnerability to addiction as an adult? Did that brief early experience of placing drugs into an "impressionable" developing brain increase the likelihood of her becoming an addict as an adult?

The developing human is certainly different from the mature human. This fact raises the likelihood that when behavioral dysfunctions appear relatively early in life (i.e., when brain, nervous system, and physiological processes have not yet fully matured), there is something remarkably different than when the same diagnosable category of illness appears in the fully mature adult. But *what* is different? It may be the case that the early-in-life onset of a disorder reflects a brain that is more vulnerable neurochemically. Or the explanation may be that the social–environmental stressors are so intense in the child or adolescent that illness will appear even without extraordinary neurochemical vulnerability. Or is it both—greater neurochemical, physiological vulnerability coupled with more intense stressors in the young? There is no definitive answer to this important question. Nevertheless, it is likely there are important differences between the child (or adolescent) and the adult who becomes behaviorally dysfunctional. Consistent with this idea is the fact that it is often case that the earlier the onset (childhood vs. adulthood) of a diagnosable behavioral disorder, the bleaker is the prospect for successful treatment and prevention of relapse.

Perspective

A useful working model holds that the likelihood that a specific category of dysfunctional behavior will develop is determined by a limited assortment of stressors interacting with a specific set of physiological or neurochemical vulnerabilities. If interacting *specific* categories of vulnerabilities and stressors cause *specific* illnesses, then we would expect that treatments for disorders ideally should *specifically* target these interacting factors.

2

What Treatments Are Likely to Be Effective?

The intense negative criticism Diane gets from her spouse so riddles her with anxiety that she has difficulty concentrating, which leads to her committing even more errors that provoke the inevitable barrage of more negative criticism. The day-time hours are manageable, but anticipation of the return of her husband from work in the early evening brings a new wave of anxiety.

From two conversations with Diane, the therapist learns that her mother was treated for obsessive–compulsive disorder (OCD; an anxiety disorder), and that Diane's life has been largely free from trauma, except for the relatively recent change in her husband's behavior—for the past 2 years he has seemed to be "angry at the world." How can the therapist best help her?

Combined Drug and Talk Treatments

If her current problem is attributable to the interaction of an inherited vulnerability toward a dysfunctional serotonin neurochemical process in the brain and the daily, chronic stressor her husband presents, a focus for Diane's therapy seems clear: Correct the neurochemical dysfunction and fix the husband. Doing only one or the other might help some, but addressing both aspects of her problem is likely to help more because it may adjust the neurochemical basis of her vulnerability *and* weaken or remove the stressor.

Removing the stressor may or may not be possible in this situation. It would likely require conversation or psychotherapy with the patient and the husband. The husband may reject being told that he is partly responsible for her problem; he may refuse to change, or he may become even angrier following the mere suggestion that he needs to change his behavior toward his wife. With or without his support, she may nonetheless benefit from some conversation that teaches her ways to cope with his anger—ways for her to still hear it but not let it debilitate her. All of this talk with her and with him may make her situation better, but a second approach may also have an impact.

The second approach would involve selecting a drug with antianxiety properties—perhaps a drug that alters serotonin neurotransmission (given her mother's history with OCD). The drug therapy will not improve her husband's bad behavior, but it may alter the way she perceives the situation and thereby diminish its negative impact upon her. The drug's ability to improve her symptoms of anxiety may be due to a drug-induced correction in the neurochemical processes related to mood; that is, the drug may do more than merely "mask" symptoms. But a chemical correction of a brain process related to mood/anxiety does not provide a long-term ideal solution to her problem if she stays married to that man. Something— probably something not drug-related—should be done to address the issue of her marriage. In summary, the best treatment likely would be a combination of talk and drug therapies.

This approach—combined drug and talk therapies to address different but related aspects of a problem—is the reasonable approach for a therapeutic program to treat a disorder presumed to be caused by an interaction of neurochemical vulnerability and environmental–social stressors. The neurochemical vulnerability factor is the factor that is perhaps best addressed by a drug that can directly change specific aspects of brain chemistry related to that specific disorder. Be cautious, however, about believing that psychotherapy *cannot* do what pharmacotherapy can do to brain chemistry. There are recent reports of psychotherapy producing changes in brain neurochemistry. Indeed, in some cases drug therapy and talk therapy appear to have strikingly similar effects on brain processes. Furthermore, drug and talk therapy do not necessarily affect change through entirely different mechanisms.

The Effectiveness of Drug Therapy

Pharmacotherapy is often presumed to be effective by changing the neurochemical vulnerability or the underlying physiological processes that contribute to symptoms. There are numerous examples, however, of a drug therapy relieving symptoms despite our near total lack of knowledge of what the drug is doing to brain neurochemistry. The most important clinical objective is to help the patient, and this may be accomplished at times without knowing exactly what a drug (or psychotherapy) is doing to brain neurochemistry.

How do we come to know whether or not a new drug will be effective in relieving symptoms? The Food and Drug Administration (FDA) has the responsibility of regulating the industries that market therapeutic drugs (and other medical procedures). A new drug can be approved for use in humans after research trials have fulfilled two conditions: (1) The drug must be evaluated in clinical trials in humans and found to be at least as effective as currently approved drugs and more effective than placebo (i.e., doing "nothing" pharmacologically), and (2) the drug must be demonstrated to be relatively safe. This condition does not mean that a drug has *no* side effects. (Any drug will have more than one effect, and therefore side effects are expected.) It does require that the benefit (main effect) of using a drug therapeutically should be judged to outweigh the risks (side effects) when that drug is compared to other treatments currently used to treat the same disorder. (Do not expect the FDA to approve only drugs that are effective and free of risks; there cannot be a drug that is free of risk, but there can be drugs that have risks worth taking for the benefits.)

Other than requiring that a new drug have demonstrated effectiveness and relative safety, the FDA does not require that the precise neurochemical mechanisms by which a drug acts be identified. Having that knowledge about a drug's neurochemical mechanism of action is certainly beneficial to a drug company's interest in developing newer, more effective drugs, but that knowledge is not essential for the effective relief of symptoms in a clinical setting.

> Rob's bipolar disorder (alternating mania and depression) has long been resistant to treatment. Nearly exasperated, Rob and his psychiatrist agree that Rob should try lamotrigine (Lamictal), a drug that has been used successfully to diminish epileptic seizures, and that has been observed anecdotally to improve symptoms in some patients with bipolar disorder. Exactly what lamotrigine is doing to brain neurochemistry to improve Rob's symptoms of bipolar disorder is not known, but the drug is now helping Rob. And that's good enough for him.

The FDA's legislated regulatory reach does not extend to chemicals classified as "dietary supplements" rather than "drugs," despite the fact that both have pharmacological properties when introduced to the brain and body. This absence of FDA oversight presents several difficulties. The paramount problem is that chemicals marketed as dietary supplements may be properly or erroneously presumed to be effective and safe, but their effectiveness and safety will *not* have been evaluated or certified by the FDA after careful evaluation of data gathered in clinical trials in humans. This situation means that a consumer is best advised that drugs approved by the FDA are more likely to be effective and relatively safe as compared to chemicals not evaluated by the FDA being sold without prescription as dietary supplements. In other words, there is generally a greater likelihood that a dietary supplement be useless and possibly harmful than is the case for an FDA-approved drug. This conclusion is a rather sweeping generalization. It may not do justice to all chemicals sold as dietary supplements, which can be purchased relatively inexpensively and without prescription, but it is a note of caution worth taking seriously.

It is also worth noting that the effectiveness of psychotherapeutic techniques is not assessed by the FDA, and that generally there is less known about the effectiveness of psychotherapeutic techniques than there is known about the effectiveness of pharmacotherapeutic agents. Research evaluating the effectiveness of nondrug therapeutic intervention is difficult to conduct. There is growing interest in conducting such studies, however, because they can assess (1) the effectiveness of psychotherapy alone, (2) the effectiveness of drug versus psychotherapy, and (3) the effectiveness of combined drug and talk approaches to either approach when used alone.

Perspective

It is reasonable to assume that the brain neurochemistry–vulnerability factors that contribute to onset and maintenance of dysfunctional behavior are the factors most pointedly treated by a therapeutic approach that directly alters brain neurochemistry—namely, a drug. Brain neurochemistry can also be altered by nondrug therapies, including psychotherapy and placebo, but those nondrug approaches generally may be assumed to be less direct ways of targeting a select change in brain neurochemistry (e.g., slowing the reuptake transport process for the neurotransmitter serotonin). Moreover, nondrug therapies may be valuable for addressing those factors that contribute to illness but are somewhat "external" to the patient, such as the patient's relationships with other people. The success of therapeutic conversations that improve social relations and therefore diminish symptoms of psychopathology does not preclude the possibility that a drug-induced alteration in perspective might also improve social relations. The chapters in Part III consider effects of drug and nondrug therapeutic approaches on brain processes for various behavioral disorders.

3

Integration of Pharmacotherapy and Psychotherapy

> Brian's symptoms of schizophrenia have improved dramatically, and it appears that he is ready to return to his parents' home. His mother and father are open to the idea. In fact, his mother is eagerly looking forward to again spending "quality time" with her son. She is certain she can offer the emotional support he needs, although Brian describes his mother's style as somewhat smothering and a little too close for comfort.
>
> What would be best for the patient? Dare he be sent home symptom-free and off of his anti-psychotic medication? Or should he be sent home with his medication, despite being symptom-free and the fact that some of the side effects of the drug are troubling? Should he receive psychotherapy upon his return home? What are the benefits of drug therapy and what are the benefits of psychotherapy? Will they duplicate or complement one another in their effectiveness?

Drugs Are Likely to Directly Alter Brain Processes

Drug therapy offers the distinct advantage of the potential to quickly and directly alter the brain neurochemical processes that are related to behavioral symptoms. Moreover, it is likely that the relief of symptoms occurs in proportion to the dosage of drug, thus permitting the option of delivering graded alterations of neurochemical substrates and relief of symptoms; this gradation might achieve a better balance between main effect and side effects, and the use of the smallest effective drug dose in combination with psychotherapy. The "direct" drug-induced alteration of brain neurochemistry related to symptoms is most likely, of course, when the drug's neurochemical mechanism of action is known to occur through the same neurochemical process that is demonstrated to underlie the symptoms.

This particular advantage of drug therapy is due to the fact that a drug has (by definition) pharmacological properties, whereas psychotherapy cannot have pharmacological properties because words are not drugs. The lack of pharmacological effects of psychotherapy does *not* mean that psychotherapy cannot have physiological or neurochemical effects, however. Therapeutic conversations that change thinking, alter perspective, or encourage learning new approaches certainly require the engagement of neurochemical processes in the brain related to cognition, emotion, and learning. Moreover, drug therapy and talk therapy have been demonstrated to alter the same neurochemical substrate in the same area of the brain in the treatment of a behavioral dysfunction (e.g., serotonin in OCD; see Chapter 10). However, it would seem that even when talk therapy can alter brain neurochemistry, it would be difficult to offer the talk in a way that produced gradations in the alteration of specific brain neurochemistry in a manner analogous to increasing or decreasing the dosage of a drug. In addition, drug therapy can quickly alter neurochemistry in rather specific regions of the brain, whereas it would seem unwise to assume that talk can have rapid effects that are so specifically localized in the brain.

The fact that a drug can directly and quickly alter brain neurochemistry suggests that it should provide more immediate relief of symptoms than would talk therapy, because drug therapy would, within minutes or hours, impact the functioning of neurons in the brain. This reasonable idea does not stand up to evidence that, in some cases (e.g., treatment of depression; see Chapter 9), the effects of a drug upon behavior are not immediate despite the fact that the drug has rather immediate, effects upon neurochemical processes.

Advantages of Drug Therapy over Psychotherapy

There are advantages of drug therapy over psychotherapy not directly related to drug's ability to alter the neurochemistry of the brain. One such advantage is that drug therapy can be a relatively discrete matter; it can be utilized in the privacy of one's own home with the knowledge of only the prescribing physician. In contrast, psychotherapy will likely require a public appearance in the waiting room of the office of a therapist who treats people who "must be crazy." Another advantage of drug therapy is that it can be relatively inexpensive, especially if the drug is available in generic form. An additional advantage of drug therapy is that, generally speaking, we might assume that drugs will act sooner—that it might take a greater length of time for talk to have its effects than for a drug to do so. It is also safe to assume that a drug therapy is generally more readily available on a day-to-day basis—it is there in our dresser drawer, and we do not need an appointment to engage it.

Advantages of Psychotherapy over Drug Therapy

Perhaps the most obvious disadvantage of drug therapy is the likelihood of side effects. Although psychotherapy may be expensive, and although it is possible that a therapist and a client can have a difficult relationship, it is not likely that psychotherapy will induce physiological or neurochemical consequences that are painful or threatening to the patient's good health (unless a client breaks out in hives at the mere sight of his or her therapist).

Psychotherapy is also advantageous because it provides opportunities to reorganize the patient's thinking, to broaden or change a perspective, or to ask the patient to willfully change his or her behavior or lifestyle in a specific way that will benefit him or her over the long term. Moreover, psychotherapy provides a way to teach skills for coping with continuing environmental or social stressors. For example, a patient can be asked to minimize daily contact with a family member who is an identifiable source of stress. Or psychotherapy can include talk with the family member who presents the source of stress; that person can be asked to change his or her behavior for the benefit of the patient.

Placebo Therapy

Placebo is neither a drug nor talk, but it is generally offered to the patient in a clinical trial (experiment) as if it were a drug. This means that although a placebo has no pharmacological properties, it may produce changes in physiology and in behavior, presumably because the patient hopes or believes that the ingested placebo (believed to be a drug) will offer relief of symptoms. Thus, placebo is more similar to talk than it is to drug, because a placebo's effect may be attributable to the fact that the patient is told to believe that it may help. We might suspect, then, that placebo treatment has the advantages and disadvantages of psychotherapy, but that is not necessarily the case. There are numerous examples, from clinical trails comparing effects of drug and placebo, of subjects receiving placebo treatment reporting "side effects" or "adverse effects" of their treatment! My personal favorite is the person in a clinical trial receiving placebo (believing it was drug) who complained of the "drug-induced" side effect of ejaculatory failure. Not to worry—the investigators conducting the clinical trial were ethically bound at the end of the trial to reveal to the guy that he was in the placebo group.

The use of placebo in a treatment program is relatively uncommon due to ethical concerns: placebo "treatment" can be viewed as the equivalent of "doing nothing," because placebo, strictly speaking, is not a drug or psychotherapy. Consequently, there is some risk in the clinical use of placebo alone, especially if it is found to have no clinical benefit for that patient. In this hypothetical situation, the patient has not been given psychotherapy, has not been given drug therapy, and has not improved. "Why not?" the patient might ask. Replying that "placebo has been demonstrated to produce changes in brain and improvement in symptoms in some clinical trials" is not an answer that would satisfy the patient, the patient's family or their lawyer. Despite this problem, it may be considered ethical to combine placebo (instead of drug) with psychotherapy in certain clinical situations, ones in which useful drug therapies carry too great a risk of side effects. For example, a woman suffering a relapse of depression early in pregnancy should not be prescribed bupropion (Wellbutrin) despite a favorable response to the drug 2 years earlier. Offering her placebo with psychotherapy, however, may produce greater relief of symptoms than psychotherapy alone.

Advantages of Combining Drug Therapy and Psychotherapy

Generally the ideal approach for improving the life of a patient may be to combine drug and talk therapy, utilizing the advantages of each and thereby minimizing the shortcomings of each. For example, for a particular disorder, it may be advantageous to initiate treatment with drug therapy to quickly diminish symptoms sufficiently to make the patient more amenable to talk therapy. That is, attempts to provide insight or new perspective may fail when offered to the delusional patient. Once drug and psychotherapy have improved the patient's conditon such that symptoms are essentially absent, it might be reasonable to end daily talk therapy but maintain drug therapy to take advantage of the potential for the drug to prevent relapse of symptoms for the patient facing continuing potent stressors. Each regimen of combined talk and drug therapies will need to be tailored to individual patients and their idiosyncratic needs. Examples are offered for some of the disorders presented in the chapters in Part III.

Perspective

Integration of pharmacotherapy and psychotherapy generally may be the ideal approach for the treatment of dysfunctional behavior, given the somewhat complementary advantages and disadvantages of drug and talk treatments, particularly when clinical research trials demonstrate that a combined therapeutic approach provides greater benefit than what can be achieved using pharmacotherapy or psychotherapy alone in the treatment of a specific disorder. Finally, the idea that pharmacotherapy alters brain neurochemistry to relieve symptoms but that psychotherapy does not alter brain neurochemistry when relieving symptoms is no longer a fair assumption.

4

Brain Theories of Behavioral Disorders

The persistent voices Paul heard in the middle of the night had become unbearable to him, and his inability to stay asleep or quiet had become unbearable to his parents. All three of them asked the psychiatrist for relief from the voices—"Please make them go away."

That appeal for help is an appeal for relief of a symptom; it is not a request for insight into the problem, it is not a request for a diagnosis or reassurance, and it most certainly is not a request for the name of a neurochemical theory for the psychosis.

Therapy-Induced Improvement in Symptoms

The visit with a clinician to seek help for a debilitating behavioral or psychological disturbance is an appeal for an improvement in the quality of life. This improvement can be accomplished even when we don't know precisely what the diagnosis should be and even when we have no explanation of exactly how the therapy is able to relieve symptoms. Those details, although interesting and potentially useful, are of secondary importance to the relief of symptoms.

It is not surprising, then, that there are situations in which the drug-induced (or psychotherapy-induced) relief of symptoms comes without an explanation of the precise mechanism of action by which a drug (or talk) relieves symptoms. That ignorance of the mechanisms of action of a therapeutic regimen does have its bright side; the fact that a drug therapy is effective provides an opportunity for the development of useful ideas.

The effectiveness of a drug in the relief of symptoms provides a point of access to learn about potential causes of the disorder. The logic is the following: If a drug improves behavioral symptoms of a psychological dysfunction, it probably does so due to its ability to change neurochemical processes in synapses in specific regions of the brain. Upon examining the neurochemical and physiological effects of that drug in experiments conducted in animals (and possibly humans), we should ultimately be able to identify the neurochemical mechanism(s) through which that drug is presumed to act to relieve symptoms. If the symptom relief is due to the changes in neurochemistry induced by the drug, it is reasonable to hypothesize that the symptoms were likely to have been caused by some disturbance in that same neurochemistry—a disturbance that happens to be corrected by the therapeutic drug.

Neurochemical Theory Relating Brain Processes to Behavioral Symptoms

Reasoning through the problem in that manner allows us to construct a tentative relation between brain neurochemical processes and dysfunctional psychological processes and behavior; in turn, this relation leads us to a rudimentary theory regarding the brain and that particular psychiatric disorder. That rudimentary theory or hypothesis is not likely to be the final word on the subject, but it provides a useful point of departure toward two goals: (1) the development of newer, better therapeutic options by which to effectively target the neurochemical abnormality in the brain; and (2) the development of a theory with better explanatory value—one that eventually could lead to even greater improvement in the clinical relief of symptoms.

How are these goals realized? Once it is discovered that a new therapeutic drug is able to block receptors for a particular neurotransmitter, it is then possible to explore the clinical potential of other drugs that have similar pharmacological properties. The importance of this exploration concerns the problem that all drugs have—that the main effect of any drug must be accompanied by one or more side effects. Drugs with a similar ability to block the same neurochemical receptors may differ in their production of unwanted side effects. Thus, having a collection of drugs with similar pharmacological properties permits some choice among alternative, imperfect options for drug therapy. In time, following extended use of such drugs in a clinical setting, it sometimes becomes clear that drugs in this group are better for relieving some symptoms than they are for improving other symptoms of that specific disorder. For example, in the case of schizophrenia, drugs that block the D2 subtype of receptor for the neurotransmitter dopamine are better at relieving some (e.g., delusions, hallucinations) but not all symptoms (e.g., anhedonia, apathy) of schizophrenia. This kind of clinical knowledge reveals some of the complexity in the problem of relating behavioral symptoms to brain neurochemical processes. What can then follow is a revised theory—one in which subsets of symptoms are related to subsets of neurochemical processes.

This revised, more nuanced theory now suggests alternative ways to proceed with the development of newer drugs, or ways in which several drugs (or drug plus psychotherapy) might be used in combination to provide more effective relief of a greater proportion of symptoms. This evolution of understanding is largely guided by experimental inquiry in animals and clinical study in humans to determine the effects of drugs upon brain processes and upon symptoms. We progress from an early, somewhat simple-minded theory relating brain processes to behavior to a somewhat more complicated and more complete theory. We consider examples of such theories in the remaining chapters of Part III.

As useful as such neurochemical theories of behavioral dysfunctions appear to be, they are not the Holy Grail of brain and behavior for two reasons:

- First, a solid theory relating a brain disorder to a behavioral dysfunction does not necessarily ensure successful clinical treatment. Parkinson's disease is a case in point: Degeneration of dopamine neurons originating in the substantia nigra and projecting to the basal ganglia are known to be the cause of Parkinson's symptoms. Despite this firm knowledge, there is no cure for Parkinson's disease; pharmacotherapy improves symptoms but does not halt the progress of this degenerating brain–behavior disorder.

- Second, a brain–behavior disorder can be successfully treated without a firm theory that relates symptoms to brain neurochemical processes. Bipolar disorder is a good case in point: The drug lamotrigine can alleviate symptoms despite our inability to track what the drug is doing to the brain neurochemistry related to those symptoms.

Perspective

Successful pharmacotherapy can lead to the development of a neuro-chemical theory relating a brain disorder to a dysfunctional behavior. Such theories generally evolve in ways that bring greater understanding of the complicated relation between multiple neurochemical processes in the brain and categories of symptoms for a specific disorder, and that advance the development of improved therapeutic approaches. A neuro-chemical theory of a dysfunctional behavior can also be misinterpreted as indicating that the dysfunctional behavior is solely caused by an inherit-ed neurochemical vulnerability. This common mistake dismisses environ-mental and social factors as secondary in importance—as only contributing factors to the psychopathology—which can lead to a second common mistake of assuming that pharmacotherapy always provides the most useful treatment. A neurochemical theory of psychopathology, properly placed, holds the disordered processes in the brain as factors that *interact with* environmental and social stressors to contribute to the likeli-hood of psychopathology.

Annotated Bibliography for Part I

The Perspectives of Psychiatry, Second Edition. McHugh, Paul R., Slavney, Phillip R. Baltimore: Johns Hopkins University Press, 1998.
This is an intelligent and provocative assessment of contemporary approaches for diagnosing and treating psychological disorders.

A Guide to Treatments That Work—Second Edition. Nathan, Peter E., & Gorman, Jack M. (Eds.). New York: Oxford University Press, 2002.
The chapters in this volume review research that assesses the efficacy of pharmacotherapeutic and psychotherapeutic approaches for treating a variety of psychological disorders.

Protecting America's Health: The FDA, Business, and One Hundred Years of Regulation. Hilts, Philip J. New York: Knopf, 2003.
This book presents the history of the business of the Food and Drug Administra-tion. It is a fascinating read that will help you understand what the FDA can and cannot do for us.

Brain Theories of Behavioral Disorders

Integrating Psychotherapy and Pharmacotherapy: Dissolving the Mind–Brain Barrier.
Beitman, Bernard D., Blinder, Barton J., Thase, Michael E., Riba, Michelle, &
Safer, Debra L. New York: Norton, 2003.
This book uses an unusual format that includes text, case study vignettes,
critique, and commentary to present a variety of issues related to the integrated
use of psychotherapy and pharmacotherapy for the treatment of behavioral
disorders. The book is quite readable, and it provides advice that can be put
into practice.

FUNDAMENTAL PRINCIPLES OF
THE BRAIN AND BEHAVIOR

Part II introduces principles regarding how neurons in the brain and peripheral nervous system are organized, and how neurochemicals act through receptors in synapses to enable neuronal systems to control behavior. Also considered are research strategies used to study the relationship between brain and behavior in animals and humans, and principles of pharmacology that are important for understanding the effective use of drugs as therapy.

5

Organizational Aspects of the Brain
Relevant to Psychology and Behavior

Each person labeled with a particular cognitive or emotional disorder is a unique individual coming from his or her own set of life circumstances and presenting his or her own idiosyncratic behaviors. Despite this uniqueness, it is possible to use the latest edition of the *Diagnostic and Statistical Manual of Mental Disorders* (DSM) to classify an individual in the best-fit diagnostic category based upon the more prominent symptoms that are featured. However convenient and useful it is to lump people into categories consistent with the DSM, assigning a single label to a category disregards the differences among the unique people assigned to that category.

Advantages of Oversimplification

Despite what is lost by fitting individuals into categories, and despite limited knowledge about all of the details in a person's brain, body, family, and social life, we categorize nonetheless, because it offers numerous practical advantages. For example, categorization facilitates communication, orients us toward the best options for treatment, and provides operational definitions that are useful in conducting research. And even though our categories are imperfect and represent oversimplifications (e.g., someone diagnosed as having an anxiety disorder may or may not also show symptoms of depression), they are used widely because oversimplification tends to fuel the confidence that is needed to get on with the business of sorting out how to best treat the problems. And treating the person is the primary problem at hand.

This tendency to oversimplify for practical advantage is also a tactic of those who teach perspectives on the organization of brain processes and their functions. For example, it remains a somewhat popular notion that the human brain is likely to have localized sites with rather specific functions, leading to ideas about the brain's "eating center" or "pleasure center", and so on. Similarly, it is common to hear speculation about the existence of a single chemical in the brain that might exclusively serve the psychological state of hunger, just as the brain might be imagined to have a single chemical that causes craving for a drug, for properly made meatballs, or for chocolate! Such simple notions about the functional organization of brain chemicals and brain locations are convenient for their simplicity, and they have their purpose when attempting to introduce the novice to the brain. But in the situation of needing to consider a meaningful perspective on organization of the brain as it relates to the rich complexity of human behaviors, it simply is not always appropriate to grossly oversimplify.

So you can expect that I, too, will use the tactic of oversimplifying to make a complex topic amenable for conversation and to give you the confidence to attempt to relate brain functions to behaviors. But I will also point out to you some of the complexity, some of the confusion, and some of the things that are *not* known. Including these parts of the overall picture will provide the opportunity for an exciting dance between what we appear to know about the human brain and what we have yet to discover about it. To set the stage for this dance, let's establish several assumptions as we begin to consider the organization of brain and nervous system:

1. Human behavior is varied and complex.
2. There are differences across gender in behaviors and in the organization of physiology and processes in the brain related to those behaviors.
3. Dysfunctional human behavior and psychological disturbances appear in a wide variety of forms, making it difficult to sharply categorize and classify the various disorders, and making it difficult to confidently assign an individual to a specific category of disorder.
4. The human brain is a magnificent assortment of cells, chemicals, and processes, many of which remain poorly understood and some of which remain unidentified, making it difficult to sharply categorize and classify the components of brain.

5. There must be a complicated relation between the processes in the brain and behavioral and psychological processes, but it is not yet possible to completely and confidently describe that relation because not enough is known about brain structures and processes, and not enough is known about how to correctly assign people to diagnostic categories.

6. All hell might break loose at any time in any number of places in the brain and physiology, resulting in dysfunctional behaviors. Thus, behavioral dysfunctions may reflect disturbances in processes that allow a person to detect, interpret, and respond emotionally to the world; dysfunctions may also reflect disturbances in processes necessary for a person to make decisions regarding how to behave; and behavioral dysfunctions may also reflect disturbances in the processes by which the brain organizes the muscles to literally move hands, legs, and lips.

With these assumptions in mind and with the understanding that difficult issues are not well served by overly simple explanations, I still nonetheless need to oversimplify somewhat in order to describe fundamental principles about the organization of brain structures, chemicals, and their behavioral functions.

> Let's say you awaken a bit earlier than usual in the morning, and walk stiffly to the kitchen. There you twice feel for the light switch, flick it up, grope for the coffee grinder and bag of beans, press the button to grind beans, holding it much too long. You place the grounds into the filter, and once you've poured water into the coffee maker, it is not long before the aroma of freshly brewed coffee alerts you to its readiness. You pour some into the cup, it warms your hands, and soon after drinking it, your head begins to clear. You are now ready for the day. What was the role of your brain and nervous system in this oft-repeated experience?

Let's begin to construct an organizational template of the brain and nervous system based upon the idea that the brain is the place where information about the world is collected, stored, and utilized. Information about the details of the immediate environment is brought to the brain through cells that are specialized for detecting aspects of the environment. These types of cells (sensory receptor cells) for the most part establish the outer reaches of the brain and nervous system: The sensory (or afferent) processes bring information from the environment to the brain (*detection*). The brain can then *integrate* and *organize* this information using cells (neurons) that are specialized for these purposes. Next, the brain can *activate* cells that coordinate activity of skeletal muscles to produce movement or behavior, and it can activate cells that coordinate activity of smooth muscle tissue to produce processes such as the gurgling of the stomach and urination. The cells that activate movement and organ function establish the other portion of the outer reaches of the brain and nervous system: These motor (or efferent) cells activate processes that act upon the environment. In summary, there are three functional components to the organization of brain and nervous system: detection, organization, and activation (Figure 5.1).

Now consider that these functions (i.e., detection, organization, activation) are arranged in a brain and nervous system that has a hierarchical structure: Sensory and motor processes, situated at the organism's perimeter in contact with its environments (external world and internal organs; Figure 5.1, Part B), can be considered the lowest elements in this hierarchy (Figure 5.2). The sensory processes are immediately reported to elements of the peripheral nervous system and the brain (Figure 5.1) that are at the bottom margin of the brain (brainstem; Figure 5.2), structures that collect sensory information before passing it to the next step in the hierarchy, where information from different sensory modalities is integrated (subcortical areas; Figure 5.2). At this point the communication among elements at the same hierarchical level is proportionately increased, facilitating the sharing of information about a variety of issues (Figure 5.2). Finally, information reaches the highest hierarchical level (cortex; Figure 5.2) where complex associations can be made.

This hierarchical structure essentially includes elements of the brain and nervous system that function as messengers, managers, and masterminds. The messenger elements can bring the relevant sensory information (e.g., the location of the light switch, the aroma of freshly brewed coffee) to the managers, without the messengers needing to discuss it much among themselves. The managers, having received the information, sort it, store it, and send it on to the appropriate masterminds; these sorting, storing, and sending tasks require some talk among managers. Once the masterminds receive the data, they interpret it and work with it

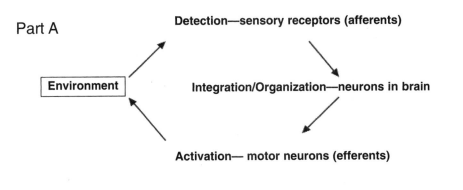

Part A

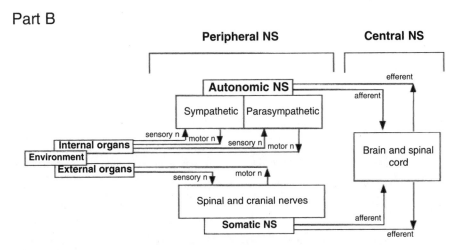

Part B

Figure 5.1 *Part A*: Schematic of the functional organization of the brain and nervous system in relation to the environment. *Part B*: Diagram identifying component sections of the peripheral and central nervous system in relation to the internal and external environments. The lines with arrows represent groups of sensory neurons or motor neurons communicating information in one or the other direction. Abbreviations: NS, nervous system; n, neurons.

to formulate a plan of action (e.g., locate and press the button to grind the coffee beans, grab the handle, pour the fluid into the mug); these tasks require considerable talk and planning among masterminds. Once a plan has been made, it is relayed to the managers, who briefly discuss arrangements for it to be executed by the messengers assigned to specific tasks (e,g., grasp the handle, smell the aroma, swallow the fluid).

The basic idea here is that there is both vertical and horizontal process-ing of sensory information (Figure 5.2): As sensory information is sent

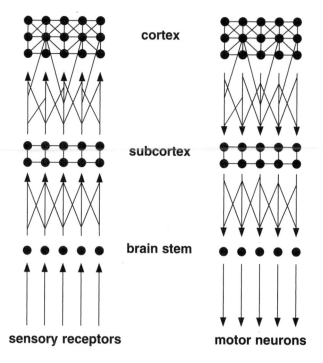

Figure 5.2 Simplified schematic of vertical and horizontal neuronal processing of ascending sensory and descending motor information at various levels of the nervous system. As sensory information ascends the hierarchy, there is greater horizontal processing of information within levels (brain stem, subcortical, cortex) of the hierarchy. An analogous situation is seen on the motor side of the diagram.

vertically, it is sent to consecutive levels in the hierarchy in which there is greater and greater horizontal communication, which permits the sharing of information. We would expect that it is at the higher hierarchical levels that the more "complex" tasks are accomplished—tasks that require integration across multiple areas and the retrieval of remembered information. Once integration is accomplished, culminating with decisions regarding movements or activities to be initiated, the organization of these motor processes proceeds from higher to lower hierarchical levels to motor elements at the outer reaches of the organism (e.g., muscles). This rather rudimentary schematic of organization is notable in its inclusion of processes above *and* below the neck, emphasizing the importance of peripheral sensory processes that gather necessary information, and those peripheral motor processes that coordinate the execution of movement.

This hierarchical organization of sensory and motor components in the brain and nervous system exists for each side of the body and each side of the brain. To a limited degree, the structures and processes on the left side of the brain (the left hemisphere) represent a mirror image of structures and processes on the right side of the brain (the right hemisphere). This mirror image does not represent a complete duplication, however; there are structural and functional differences between the left and right cerebral hemispheres of the brain—sometimes referred to as a *laterality* of structures and functions. Perhaps the best example of laterality of structure and function across the cerebral hemispheres is the fact that, for the vast majority of right-handed people, the lateral areas of the cerebral cortex within the left hemisphere of the brain are "dominant" for language. The lateral regions of the cortex in the right hemisphere certainly serve the various functions of communication, but the cortex within the right hemisphere is, relatively speaking, less important for language than is the temporal cortex in the left hemisphere. Another way to illustrate this point is to consider the functional deficit that would follow damage to either one of these areas in the human brain: A person sustaining damage to a specific region of the left cortex might suffer near total loss of the ability to speak in sentences. If that person instead sustained damage to the identical area of cortex in the right cerebral hemisphere, there may be little or no loss of the ability to speak.

Laterality of structures and functions is not unique to the cortex and language. Laterality is a fundamental principle of how structures in the brain and nervous system integrate information that will be used to organize functions. This integration of information is (for the most part) accomplished by cells specialized for the role—these specialized cells are the neurons.

Neuron: The Fundamental Functional Unit of the Brain and Nervous System

A neuron is only one type of cell among the many types of cells that are found in the brain. Although there are various types of non-neuronal cells that support processes (e.g., circulation of blood in the brain, repair to damaged neurons) that are related, in some indirect ways, to a person's ability to think, feel, and behave, the neuron is notable for its central role in the processing and communication of information. The integration of information about the immediate environment and about learned and remembered aspects of that world are of central importance for the animal's and the human's ability to act appropriately in that environment. Therefore, cells that specialize in receiving and communicating information appear to contribute in an essential way to an individual's ability to function behaviorally (and physiologically). So, although a neuron cannot survive without the performance of cells that support it (i.e., by bringing it necessary fuels such as glucose and oxygen), these non-neuronal cells can be considered of secondary importance for behavior, whereas neurons are considered to be of primary importance for behavior.

That is easily said, but it is more difficult to imagine exactly how neurons go about their business of organizing behavior when we realize that there are literally many billions of neurons in a single adult human brain. Moreover, it is difficult to envision how these billions of neurons are physically arranged when we see the various and complicated shapes and sizes that neurons present upon examination, and when we see that adjacent neurons may have numerous (not single) points of contact for interaction with one another. In fact, perhaps the most honest description of the apparent physical arrangement of these billions of neurons in the brain would be to portray it as a hopelessly tangled mess of neurons of different shapes and sizes communicating with one another. It is this hopelessly tangled mess that is assumed to be functioning in a way that keeps behaviors organized. So how can we go about disentangling this mess of neurons to sort out functional relationships between specific neurons and specific psychological processes and behaviors?

Those who study the brain have imposed their own ideas of a system of organization upon a structure (brain) that appears to be something entirely too complicated to sort out. For example, we could begin by assuming that there are groups and subgroups of neurons; we could further assume that specific subgroups of neurons may serve specific behavioral functions.

This approach of assigning functions to specific groups of neurons has been, and continues to be, useful (despite some limitations). The first attempts at "grouping" neurons in this way brought us (in the middle part of the 20th century) the notion of "centers" in the brain for specific functions. For example, the "hunger center" was believed to be the specific area of the brain identified as the lateral hypothalamus. This type of simplistic idea about functional organization was quite naïve because it assumed that the specific anatomical location(s) of neurons was the sole determinant of those neurons' function(s). This assumption excluded the possibility that different neurons in the same place might be using quite different means of communication. For example, different neurons in the same place might be using different chemicals to communicate with one another.

The hallmark behavioral symptoms of Parkinson's disease include tremor, difficulty initiating movements, a rigid manner of walking (as if one's knees won't bend). These symptoms are somewhat familiar to many of us owing to the fact that some celebrity Parkinson's patients (e.g., actor Michael J. Fox) have publicly championed the cause of research to discover new therapies. These symptoms are known to appear and gradually worsen as a particular group of neurons in the brain continues to degenerate and die. Those neurons are located in a particular place in the brain within the hierarchy of motor neurons that manage movement. Moreover, those degenerating neurons belong to a subgroup of a larger group of neurons that use the chemical dopamine to accomplish their functions.

Neurochemicals: The Fundamental Messengers Conveying Neuronal Information

This tangled mess of neurons uses chemicals to communicate between and among neurons. Please note that I have avoided saying that one neuron communicates with the next neuron by using a single chemical messenger to make that contact. It is more complicated than that.

To begin with, there are various categories of neurochemicals—that is, chemicals that are used in the brain and nervous system to communicate information. One category, the hormones, includes chemicals that travel in the blood to communicate information across great distances (e.g., between brain and kidney). Another category, the neurotransmitters, is best known for its role in mediating communication among neurons. A neurotransmitter is a chemical released by a neuron so that this chemical can have an effect upon an adjacent neuron or many adjacent neurons. But be careful with the image you have of this process! You should have an image that includes the likelihood that a single neuron can release numerous different types of neurotransmitter chemicals. Your image should include the idea that different amounts of each neurotransmitter substance might be released at different points in time. Finally, your image should not include the reasonable but too simple notion that it is the type of chemical released that determines the specific outcome or function, because just as a single neuron is not likely to be related to a single behavior, so too a single chemical neurotransmitter is not likely to have a single behavioral function. This is so because in order for a neurotransmitter chemical to exert its function it must interact with chemical receptors.

Receptors: The Fundamental Chemical Unit That Determines Functions

The chemical neurotransmitter released by a neuron is permitted to function as it interacts with various other chemical units, called *receptors*, which are located on adjacent neurons. There can be numerous "subtypes" of these receptors, each which permits the neurotransmitter chemical to execute one or several of its functions. What is interesting and useful about this arrangement is that it permits a single neurotransmitter chemical released by a neuron to have multiple functions or outcomes, because its functions are a consequence of the interaction of a single neurotransmitter with multiple subtypes of receptors. (Again, its functions are *not* a consequence of merely the identity of the released chemical neurotransmitter.)

Thus far we've considered three fundamental points about the organization of neurons in brain:

- *Neurons* are the cells that are specialized for communication.
- *Neurotransmitters* are chemicals released by neurons to initiate commerce with other neurons.
- *Receptors* interact with the neurotransmitters released by the neurons, and it is this interaction that permits the functions of a neuron's neurotransmitters.

It would be useful now to take these three units—neuron, neurotransmitters, receptors—and place them in an organizational scheme. How are these units organized in the brain?

Neuroanatomists who study the structure of the brain have described arrangements of neurons in systems or networks that have quite predictable locations from one brain to another. These map-like descriptions of neuroanatomy include the origin and destination of neurons, which are often arranged in groups of hundreds or thousands that transmit information from one area to other areas of the brain (Figure 5.3). One group or bundle of neurons need not be entirely distinct from another group or bundle; in fact, groups may overlap and interact. Thus, a group of neurons serving some function may also serve a second function by interacting with an adjacent group of neurons. The basic idea here is that the neuroanatomy or circuitry of the brain is one way in which neurons are organized to serve various functions. That is, the location of neurons in the brain *to* some extent determines the functions of those neurons.

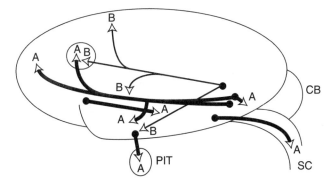

Figure 5.3 Diagram of neurons in two (hypothetical) interacting neurotransmitter systems: The thicker black lines represent bundles of neurons utilizing neurotransmitter A; the thinner black lines represent bundles of neurons utilizing neurotransmitter B. The white arrows indicate the terminal portions of those bundles of neurons at the sites in brain where neurotransmitters A or B will be released to interact with receptors in synapses. Note that neurons using transmitter B are arranged in a manner suggesting that neurotransmitter system B can modulate the activity of neurotransmitter system A. Note also that there is a site in the brain (circled A and B together) in which both neurotransmitters A and B are released. Abbreviations: PIT, pituitary; CB, cerebellum; SC, spinal cord. This drawing is a view from the side of only the left hemisphere of the brain. The structures of the brain are represented in each of the two hemispheres.

Now remind yourself that neurons release chemical neurotransmitters to communicate, and you will remember that a group of neurons in a specific place in the brain is likely to have different neurons using numerous, different chemical neurotransmitters, and that some of these chemicals may be more abundant in some places in the brain than in other places. For example, a bundle of neurons with a specific origin and a specific destination may include a sizable proportion of neurons that use a specific chemical transmitter to communicate. If you think about this a bit, you can see that the arrangement of neurons in a kind of circuitry (or neuroanatomy) must include some chemical identification, because neurons use chemicals to communicate. Given this fact, we can talk about many groups of neurons (or systems) in the brain by referring to them by the name of the specific chemical transmitter or transmitters that these neurons utilize. Thus, the brain can also organize its functions by virtue of the fact that neurons in specific locations in the brain release specific neurochemicals.

Finally, remind yourself that these chemical transmitters, released by neurons in specific places in the brain, are acting through receptors located in those specific places. With this in mind, you can imagine that neurochemists and neuroanatomists together should be able to provide maps of where in the brain specific subtypes of receptors can be found, and that the identification of the location of these receptors also reveals useful information about how the brain's neurons and neurochemicals organize behavior.

Let's piece this all together and see what we can say about the functional organization of neurons in the brain: The brain contains neurons arranged in specific, overlapping, interacting circuits that can be defined by the chemical transmitters and the chemical receptors that are utilized by the neurons. Thus, one large group of neurons in a specific location in the brain may include neurons that use neurotransmitter A to interact with three subtypes of receptors (subtypes 1A, 2A, and 3A) to organize functions X, Y, Z, and more. This arrangement allows a specific chemical in the brain and a specific location in the brain to serve multiple functions.

Now you may be thinking "Well, that's all superbly fascinating, but how does it explain why a chicken can still walk around once its head has been cut off?" That chicken without its brain attached is walking around because it has a spinal cord and a peripheral nervous system that is adequate to keep it moving (for a short time, at least). That's a pretty impressive accomplishment for a spinal cord and peripheral nervous system—but perhaps that accomplishment might be expected if we considered the thousands of neurons, neurochemicals, and receptors that are to be found below the neck.

There is an anatomy and a chemistry of neurons below the neck that serve the sensory and motor processes of the peripheral nervous system (Figure 5.1), including the autonomic nervous system (Figure 5.4), and there is a rich peripheral physiology that is important for psychological processes and behavior. The brain uses neurons and neurochemicals to coordinate activities in the periphery. It is equally important to note that the brain is also immediately informed (through sensory, afferent neurons, and neurochemicals) of the activities of organs in peripheral physiology. So intimate is this relation between brain and below-the-neck processes that it is useful to consider that brain and peripheral neurons and physiology together contribute to behavior and psychological processes. Let's look at one example.

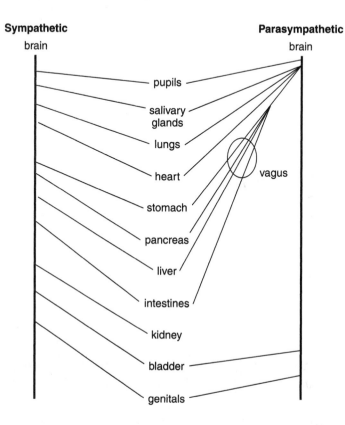

Figure 5.4 Schematic diagram of the sympathetic and parasympathetic segments of the peripheral autonomic nervous system. Long vertical lines represent spinal cord and spinal ganglia. All other lines represent bundles of neurons, each of which contains neurons carrying information from organs to brain (sensory; afferent) and from brain to organs (motor; efferent). The abdominal vagus portion of cranial nerve X, important for physiological processes related to eating behavior, is circled.

Case Study: Brain, Physiology, Hunger, Eating Behavior, and Satiety

Humans readily identify the feeling of hunger and have little difficulty imagining that the perception of hunger (apart from the physiology of hunger itself) is a process in the brain. At the same time we would readily admit that below-the-neck sensations, such as growling of the stomach, are very much a part of our perception of being hungry. Once we begin to eat, the perception of hunger gradually diminishes; that annoying growling in the stomach ends, some pleasant sensations take place in the mouth, and there may be some feelings of fullness in the stomach (especially if we eat too much).

Although this description captures only a fraction of the feelings or perceptions associated with hunger, eating, and satiety, it is fairly easy to see how eating behavior motivated by hunger and having the consequence of satiety represents a set of processes organized by the brain and peripheral nervous system and physiology. So how do the brain and nervous system and physiology accomplish this coordination?

Our current understanding of the hunger and satiety cycle is incomplete, but it has improved greatly over the past 50 years. The development of our understanding has been aided by the identification of "new" (i.e., previously unknown) neurochemicals in the brain and below the neck, and a more sophisticated appreciation of how the brain and peripheral processes work together. A brief historical look at the conceptualization of the brain's control of eating will help us appreciate the complexity of the relation between the brain and behavior.

The earliest (1950s–1960s) conceptualization of how the brain organizes hunger and eating considered that there was likely to be a "hunger center" and possibly a "satiety center" in the brain. The hunger center, identified as the lateral hypothalamus, was viewed as having cells that were able to detect diminished sources of chemical fuel (e.g., glucose); the detection of fuel deficits was considered to provoke feelings of hunger, which in turn would lead to eating behavior that would repair the deficits in fuels. Once eating commenced, the "satiety center," identified as the ventromedial hypothalamus situated near the lateral hypothalamus "hunger center," was viewed as having cells that were able to detect replenishment of fuel supplies (e.g., an increase in the concentration of glucose in the blood; filling of the stomach). The detection of replenishment was considered to provoke feelings of satiety, which would lead to a slowing and eventually stopping of eating behavior. That conceptualization was nice and tidy: two processes (hunger and satiety), two closely related areas of the brain, and each area serving one process. This hypothesis about how brain organized eating behavior began to tarnish in the face of research of various kinds, including research that identified greater details about the neurochemistry and neuroanatomy of the brain.

One point that soon became clear was that an area such as the lateral hypothalamus did not simply serve a limited purpose. In fact, the lateral hypothalamus was discovered to be an area across which many neurons traversed—neurons with origins and destinations well beyond the perimeters of the lateral hypothalamus. The same was discovered to be true about the ventromedial hypothalamus. It also became clear that some of the neurons passing through in these areas of the hypothalamus were utilizing specific chemical neurotransmitters such as dopamine, serotonin, and norepinephrine. This new information about neuroanatomy and neurochemistry began to make these hypothalamic areas of the brain look less like "centers" with limited, isolated functions and more like complex areas in which information from a wide variety of chemically defined systems of neurons is gathered, processed, and passed on.

Another attractively simple notion that a single neurochemical might signal hunger or satiety met with contrary evidence showing that experimental manipulations in chemical systems such as dopamine, serotonin, and norepinephrine, located both inside *and* outside of the hypothalamus, could dramatically affect hunger and change eating behavior. These kinds of research findings identified multiple neurochemical systems— systems in the brain that were large and that served the hypothalamus as well as regions of the brain nowhere near the hypothalamus—as having roles in hunger and eating.

Accompanying these findings, which suggested that numerous areas of the brain and numerous chemicals in the brain were likely to be involved in hunger and eating, were findings that demonstrated the importance of neurons and chemicals in the peripheral nervous system and physiology. For example, it became apparent that not only did the hypothalamus in the brain have cells or neurons capable of detecting a decline in availability of glucose, but so too did the liver. It also became clear that the ability of the hypothalamus to receive signals regarding the emptiness or fullness of the stomach depended upon neurons in the autonomic nervous system outside of the brain (Figure 5.4)—sensory (afferent) neurons that relayed information from the stomach to the brain, so that the brain had the information it needed to use motor (efferent) neurons to appropriately control the functioning of the stomach. These types of findings made clear that there were physiological events below the neck that were important for the ability of various areas of the brain to organize eating behavior.

Failure to confirm the delightfully simple notions of one hunger center in the brain, one hunger neurochemical in the brain, one satiety center, and one satiety neurochemical, was accompanied by research findings identifying a growing list of peripheral neurochemicals that could signal satiety for food. One of the earliest of these identified was cholecystokinin, a chemical found in the small intestine. This chemical can be released from cells in the intestine when food that had been eaten only minutes before has made its way from the mouth to the stomach and then to the intestine. This eating-induced release of cholecystokinin provides a signal relayed to the brain by the vagus nerve (Figure 5.4) to stop eating. The evidence supporting the idea that a below-the-neck chemical such as cholecystokinin could act as a satiety signal for the brain has been followed by findings identifying a still-growing list of such peripheral chemical signals for satiety (see Chapter 12).

So what has finally happened to the notion of one or a few areas of the brain and one or a few chemicals in the brain controlling hunger and satiety? It's become a dumb idea. It's too simple a notion to fit the facts of the research findings, despite it's desirability in terms of offering an elegant solution. For example, wouldn't it be nice to be able to say to the person diagnosed with anorexia nervosa that we can solve the anorexia part of her problem with a drug that simply activates the hunger center or the hunger neurochemical in the brain? Wouldn't it be just as nice to say to the person diagnosed with bulimia that we can solve the binge eating part of her problem with a drug that diminishes the activity of that same hunger center or that hunger neurochemical? But, alas, the brain and its relation to the peripheral nervous system and peripheral physiology are too complex to permit such simple solutions.

Having no simple solution that completely remedies a problem does not preclude having a useful solution of some kind. Let's stay with a consideration of anorexia nervosa and bulimia: A glance at the DSM diagnostic criteria for these disorders reveals that the person's problems are greater than simply eating too little or too much (see Chapter 13). The richness and complexity of the psychological disturbances and the behavioral abnormalities of disorders such as these (and others such as anxiety, psychosis, and depression) should not be expected to match up neatly to a single area of the brain or a single neurochemical in the brain. It makes more sense to expect a rich, complicated state of dysfunction in the brain and peripheral physiology accompanying the rich assortment of behavioral and psychological issues presented by the anorexic or the bulimic. It may be more difficult to completely understand the relation between such complexity in brain and disarray in behavior when it is a complicated relation, but the complex nature of the relation does not preclude progress. A suitable understanding of a mere fraction of the complex equation may be sufficient to permit a novel and effective clinical approach to a problem. For example, administration of a drug such as fluoxetine (Prozac), which is relatively selective for altering the functioning of the neurotransmitter serotonin, can improve some symptoms in some people with bulimia. This clinical improvement is real, measurable, and clinically meaningful despite lacking an explanation of precisely *why* fluoxetine would have this effect.

It is fortunate to be able to make progress in the clinical treatment of psychological and behavioral disorders despite being relatively ignorant about how the brain and nervous system organize behaviors. Indeed, a precise and complete understanding of the brain's control of human behavior will not be forthcoming anytime soon. Why? Because the human brain is a great frontier, largely undescribed and unexplored because it has not yet been possible to identify all of its neurochemicals. A reasonable estimate is that much less than 25% of the neurochemistry of the brain has been identified. So experimental research that studies the relation of brain to behavior must be limited to that relatively small fraction of the brain and its neurochemistry that *has* been identified and that *can* be manipulated and measured in research.

Perspective

Let's review briefly what can be said to provide a broad perspective about how the brain and peripheral processes may organize a behavior as simple as eating. The brain contains multiple areas and neurochemicals that are important for eating and relatively few specific systems of neurons that use numerous yet specific neurochemicals important for eating. The brain receives sensory information from the external environment and from peripheral organs and chemicals. These peripheral signals are transmitted to the brain by peripheral neurons using neurotransmitters or hormones. These peripheral signals play an important role in the brain's ability to organize eating behavior. Thus, hunger and satiety are processes that depend upon neurons in brain, peripheral neurons and physiology, and numerous chemicals in the brain as well as in the periphery.

This complicated picture may be representative of the way in which the brain, nervous system, and physiology organize numerous behaviors. There is no simplicity in that picture, but there are particular aspects of this incompletely understood picture that provide windows of opportunity for understanding the relation between brain and behavior in a way that facilitates understanding and treatment of psychological and behavioral disorders.

When attempting to understand the relation between a disordered brain and dysfunctional behavior, it is useful to consider that the numerous processes in the brain, nervous system, and physiology that function in relation to a specific behavior or psychological process are *all* candidates as sites of the malfunctioning leading to the dysfunctional behavior. The sites of malfunctioning for a particular disorder could be within sensory (afferent) processes of the somatic or autonomic nervous system (Figure 5.1), leading to deficiencies in the quality or quantity of information from the environment that is provided to the brain—for example, the loss of sensory information from cells in the retina of the eye (in macular degeneration) that leads to behavioral adaptations to cope with the diminished visual acuity. On the other hand, sensory processes may remain normally functional, but abnormal functioning of neurons and neurochemicals within the brain itself could lead to misinterpretation or mishandling of the sensory information—for example, the abnormal processing of visual information by subcortical and cortical areas of brain that leads to reading disorders (dyslexias). Then again, sensory and interpretive processes may remain normally functional, but motor (efferent) processes that coordinate and activate behavior and physiology may be abnormal—for example, the degeneration of dopamine neurons serving the subcortical caudate nucleus and putamen that results in the abnormal movements symptomatic of Parkinson's disease. And a further possibility is that dysfunctional behavior and psychological processes could, at times, result from combined disorders in sensory, integrative, and motor processes of the brain and peripheral nervous system, as might be the case in anxiety disorders (Chapter 10). Identifying the sites of malfunctioning within the organization of the brain and nervous system is an important step toward a plan for successful treatment. Let's now begin to look more closely at some of the details of the brain and nervous system that are most relevant to familiar and important clinical issues.

6

Neuronal Processes Relevant to Psychology and Behavior

Those responsible for treating psychological disorders cannot ignore the relevance and importance of the neurons and associated processes that are related to behavior. This opinion should appear reasonable after a brief look at perhaps the best-known tale of success regarding the pharmacological treatment of a disabling mental disorder—the use of drugs to treat schizophrenia. There are various ways to tell this story; I'll structure the story to show how it contains the familiar steps involved in the process of discovering novel treatments for known disorders.

The Story of a Successful Drug

• *First step in the process of discovery*: It is not unusual to discover somewhat by accident that a particular drug can be used to successfully treat patients who previously had been unresponsive to treatment. For example, chlorpromazine (Thorazine) was found in the mid 1950s to relieve some symptoms of schizophrenia in some patients. This finding was unexpected; chlorpromazine was being tested to investigate its sedative properties (not its antipsychotic properties). Other examples of serendipitous drug discoveries from the 1940s and 1950s include: (a) finding the antianxiety properties of mephenesin, meprobamate (Miltown), and chlordiazepoxide (Librium) while searching for antibacterial agents; (b) discovering the antidepressant effects of iproniazid while searching for antitubercular agents; and (c) detecting the antidepressant effects of imipramine after it failed to demonstrate antipsychotic utility.

• *Second step in the process*: A new treatment might be used clinically despite lack of understanding of how or why it is successful. In the case of chlorpromazine, there was at least a decade of successful clinical usage before it was known that chlorpromazine blocked a subtype of receptors for a specific neurotransmitter (dopamine), thus disrupting the functioning of dopamine neurons in the brain.

• *Third step in the process*: The success of the novel therapeutic approach together with the new understanding of how the approach alters the functioning of the brain usually leads to a new neurochemical theory for the disorder. In the case of chlorpromazine (and other anti-schizophrenic drugs), it led to the "dopamine theory" for schizophrenia in the 1970s and 1980s, a theory that related symptoms to dopamine neurons and receptors.

• *Fourth step in the process*: The details of the new theory often lead to development of newer, better drugs due to basic research in animals and clinical research in humans. In the case of antipsychotic drugs, we have dozens of older-generation drugs such as chlorpromazine and haloperidol (Haldol), and we now have newer-generation antipsychotics such as risperidone (Risperdol) and clozapine (Clozaril).

• *Fifth step in the process*: Following more research and clinical experience, the new neurochemical theory for a disorder is inevitably found to be overly simplistic, resulting in its continuing refinement and in the development of another set of novel clinical approaches for treatment.

This course of progress from serendipitous discovery of a new drug treatment to new conceptualizations about brain and behavior has at its foundation (1) a group of behavioral symptoms that warrant relief; (2) the discovery of a novel therapeutic approach; (3) success of the therapeutic approach in revealing how the functioning of neurons in the brain is disordered; and (4) a new knowledge about the brain that facilitates a search for newer, more effective ways of altering the dysfunctional neurons to relieve the behavioral symptoms.

This scenario invites the curious to wonder what areas of the brain and which neurochemical processes in the brain underlie normal and dysfunctional behaviors. What brain processes are most directly engaged in detecting and perceiving our world, integrating that collected information, and activating a behavioral response to the environment? And how can these processes, when they have become disordered, be corrected by pharmacotherapy or psychotherapy?

Neurons: Structure and Processes Related to Behavior

Let's start with neurons to begin a closer look at the brain processes that are relevant to behavior, and let's assume that it makes good sense to describe one neuron as being representative of the billions of neurons in a single brain. Now that is a rather large assumption, but it provides a reasonable place to begin. So let's consider the "typical" neuron, keeping in mind that this is somewhat like considering that Bucky Kat, in the comic strip "Get Fuzzy," can represent all of the male and female cats in the world. Even though Bucky Kat is unique as a cartoon male cat, he embodies enough of the essence of "catness" that we can see in Bucky much that is true about all cats. This statement may not quite be fair to all cats out there, but it is useful and fun to consider that Bucky is the typical cat.

The typical neuron (our cartoon version) must be capable of receiving and processing information if its fundamental role is communication. Let's identify only those structures and processes that are necessary for neurons to be able to accomplish communication. We need to consider the following structures for our typical neuron: dendrites, receptors, cell body (soma), axon, axon terminal, and synapse (Figure 6.1). Within this list of structures, we need to consider the following processes: synthesis and storage of neurotransmitter(s); release of neurotransmitter(s) to permit its interaction with receptors in the synapse; and recovery or removal of released neurotransmitter(s).

Dendrites are generally the structures on neurons that receive information from other neurons, and the receptors on dendrites are the chemical structures that are directly engaged in that communication. If a neuron is to have the ability to receive, virtually simultaneously, many and various kinds of information from dozens, hundreds, or even thousands of other neurons, then it is likely that there will need to be many dendrites on a single neuron, and it is likely that these dendrites will need many receptors and multiple kinds of them to gather information from numerous different chemical transmitters. The receptors on dendrites are available to interact with neurotransmitters released by other neurons that are sending information to the dendrites of that neuron receiving the information. It is this transmitter–receptor interaction on dendrites that excites the neuron receiving the message to perform its communicative function. The bottom line is that receptors on dendrites are important for receiving information from other neurons.

Once this information is received by a neuron, it must be processed for that neuron to have an impact upon adjacent neurons. That processing or integration of information takes place, generally speaking, along dendrites in a manner that integrates a mix of excitatory and inhibitory signals (Figure 6.1). These excitatory and inhibitory events are defined as such by the chemical characteristics of the transmitter–receptor interactions; some transmitter–receptor interaction events produce excitation of

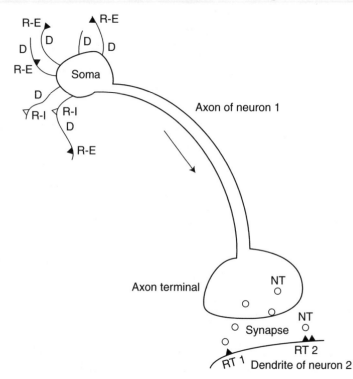

Figure 6.1 Drawing of the essential parts of the "typical" neuron. Arrow indicates direction of the action potential along the axon. R-E and R-I represent excitatory and inhibitory receptors on dendrites (D) for interacting with neurotransmitters released from other neurons. Open circles (NT) are neurotransmitter molecules released from the axon terminal into the synapse to interact with RT1 and RT2 subtypes of receptors on the dendrite of neuron 2.

the membrane of dendrites, other transmitter–receptor interaction events produce inhibition of the dendritic membrane. Whether or not an event is excitatory or inhibitory depends upon the specific neurotransmitters and receptors that are interacting. If the combination of excitatory and inhibitory events reaches some minimal threshold value of excitation, then the neuron whose dendrites are receiving this mix of excitatory and inhibitory events will be sufficiently stimulated to send its own message to other adjacent neurons.

That message will be sent along the axon of the neuron, beginning at the place where the axon joins the cell body (soma). The message that travels along the axon to its terminal is called the *action potential*. This action potential is perhaps best considered to be a traveling impulse that reflects the electrical and chemical changes occurring along the axon of the neuron. This electrochemical impulse is a major event for a neuron—it is the event or process that is required for that neuron to send its own message to other neurons. The action potential itself is an interesting and complicated process in terms of its electrical and chemical properties—but action potentials tend not to fascinate psychologists! Nonetheless, action potentials are important to even disinterested psychologists for several reasons:

• First, without the action potential there would be no communication from that neuron to the next neurons.

• Second, the fact that an action potential occurs *only if* a neuron is sufficiently excited by other neurons represents a mechanism by which a neuron only speaks when it has something important to say: Action potentials don't just occur spontaneously; they occur in response to an appropriate integration of excitatory and inhibitory events in that single neuron. Action potentials represent an ability of a neuron to reveal that it has been addressed by a specific group of other neurons in a fairly specific manner through the interactions of neurotransmitters and receptors.

• Third, action potentials occur rapidly and frequently. An action potential occurs in milliseconds (i.e., thousandths of a second) and can occur so frequently that it is reasonable to measure changes in rates of action potentials for a single neuron. These different rates of action potentials occurring for a single neuron can enrich the manner in which a single neuron communicates with others: For example, consider that the same neuron can send two different messages simply due to an alteration in the number of action potentials taking place in it across time.

• Finally, the action potential is important because of its consequence: When the action potential travels the length of the axon and reaches the axon terminal, the neurotransmitter(s) that has been synthesized and stored in vesicles is released to send a message to the next neuron. It is this primary consequence of an action potential—the release of chemical neurotransmitters—that is so very important and so interesting to even psychologists. This release of neurotransmitter(s), which occurs in proportion to the rate at which the neuron is processing action potentials, sends the chemical message that will interact with receptors on the next neuron(s). And it is this chemical transmitter–receptor interaction that will either excite or inhibit the dendrites of the next neurons, determining whether or not that neuron then becomes sufficiently excited to have its own action potential.

We've come full circle. I began by describing how the release of neurotransmitter interacts with receptors on dendrites of a neuron . . . which determines whether or not that neuron is sufficiently excited to have its own action potential . . . which releases neurotransmitter to interact with receptors on dendrites of other neurons . . . which determines whether or not those neurons are sufficiently excited to have their own action potentials. If we play with this scenario for a considerable while, extending it to more and more neurons beyond the one neuron where we started, we would be describing activity throughout the billions of neurons in the human brain. The bottom line: Neurons communicate with one another by being stimulated by other neurons and, in turn, by stimulating other neurons. The key process in this network of communication events is the interaction of the released chemical transmitter with receptors on the adjacent neuron. This key neurochemical–receptor interaction occurs in the space between adjacent neurons: the synapse.

Synapse: Venue for Chemical Interactions between Neurons

The synapse provides the venue in which neurochemicals, released from axon terminals of neurons, have the opportunity to interact with various subtypes of receptors on dendrites of adjacent neurons (Figure 6.2). This chemical interaction, sometimes characterized as the "binding" of released neurotransmitters to receptors, is the key event that permits communication among neurons in the brain and in the peripheral nervous system. These binding events, occurring among the billions of neurons in the brain, contribute to the integration of information related to psychological processes and behaviors.

These synaptic events can be facilitated or disrupted; they can be amplified or diminished. For example, the fact that these synaptic events can be attenuated or blocked by drugs that relieve symptoms of schizo-

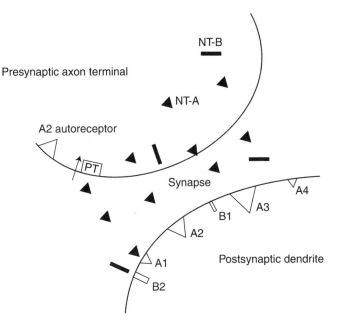

Figure 6.2 Schematic drawing of a synapse between a presynaptic axon terminal and a postsynaptic dendrite. A black triangle is a molecule of neurotransmitter NT-A; a black rectangle is a molecule of neurotransmitter NT-B. An open triangle is an A1, A2, A3, or A4 receptor subtype, which can bind to neurotransmitter NT-A. An open rectangle is a B1 or B2 receptor subtype, which can bind to neurotransmitter NT-B. The rectangle PT is the presynaptic transporter for NT-A reuptake.

phrenia led to the notion that symptoms of schizophrenia may represent disturbances in transmitter–receptor interactions. It is that kind of fact that makes synaptic processes so important and so interesting to psychologists: The synapse may be the best target for therapeutic alterations of processes gone haywire; transmitter–receptor interactions are certainly vulnerable to manipulation by drug therapy, and they also may be vulnerable to alteration by psychotherapy.

In fact, for several decades now, the synapse has been a focal point for thinking about how chemicals in the brain are related to psychological processes and behaviors. Indeed, the chemistry of synapses has been assumed to be the very hub of brain chemistry–behavior interactions. The chemical processes that occur in synapses have been assumed to be the ones most relevant to the actions of psychoactive drugs in altering psychological processes and behavior.

The synapse (Figure 6.2), a small gap between the axon terminal of the neuron sending the message (the presynaptic neuron) and the dendrite of the neuron receiving the message (the postsynaptic neuron), receives neurotransmitters delivered by the axon terminal when the action potential has arrived at the terminal. The delivery of this transmitter into the synaptic gap (or synaptic cleft) positions the transmitter molecules to interact with receptors of various subtypes on the postsynaptic dendrite. Moreover, this same released neurotransmitter can also find in the synapse the opportunity to interact with receptors on the presynaptic axon terminal—that is, receptors on the very neuron that just released the transmitter chemical. Keeping in mind that a single variety of neurochemical transmitter can interact with numerous subtypes of chemical receptors, we can see that the synapse is a place where multiple consequences of a single variety of neurochemical transmitter can be realized. By multiple functions I do not mean multiple behaviors, however. No single transmitter–receptor interaction in a single synapse for a single chemical in a human brain will entirely control some single behavior, but there can be multiple functions or consequences of neurotransmitter–receptor interactions in one synapse.

For example, let's consider a fictitious representative neurotransmitter called neurotransmitter A (Figure 6.2). Let's assume neurotransmitter A is the type of neurotransmitter that can interact with four subtypes of receptors, called subtypes A1, A2, A3, and A4. The release of neurotransmitter A into a synapse provides molecules of neurotransmitter A with access to each of the four subtypes of receptors, assuming that the A1, A2, A3, and A4 subtypes are available at that point in time. (We'll read more on the issue of availability a little later.) Let's say that neurotransmitter A binds with a subtype A1 receptor in the membrane of the postsynaptic dendrite, and when it does so the consequence is an event that is excitatory to that dendrite. As neurotransmitter A binds with a subtype A2 receptor, the consequence is also an excitatory event on the membrane of the postsynaptic dendrite. These excitatory events, each a consequence of transmitter A interacting with two unique receptor subtypes (A1 and A2), will increase the likelihood that the receiving neuron, the postsynaptic neuron, will be sufficiently excited to begin having its action potential. Now let's add to the synaptic mix the idea that neurotransmitter A, as it interacts with the subtype A3 receptor, has an effect that is quite the opposite—the transmitter A and receptor subtype A3 interaction produces an inhibitory event that *decreases* the likelihood that the postsynaptic neuron will begin its action potential. If these events were to occur together simultaneously—A interacting with receptor A1, A interacting with receptor A2, and A interacting with receptor A3—the ultimate consequence will be some mix of excitatory and inhibitory events. As long as the inhibitory events do not greatly diminish or completely negate the excitatory events, the postsynaptic neuron may be sufficiently excited to have its action potential.

Now let's also consider that neurotransmitter A can interact with receptor subtype A4, but that such an interaction will have an excitatory consequence *only if* neurotransmitter B is also present in the synapse. This kind of situation illustrates how two neurotransmitters released from the same neuron into the same synapse can interact in a way that suggests that neurotransmitter B (through its interaction with subtype B receptors) "permits" the ability of neurotransmitter A to activate a process through receptor subtype A4. Things can get complicated in a synapse, what with multiple neurotransmitters being released and numerous subtypes of receptors awaiting the various types of neurotransmitters!

Let's step away from the details of the above examples for a moment and consider the general principles illustrated by them:

- First, several different neurochemicals can be released into a single synapse.
- Second, a neurotransmitter can activate multiple subtypes of receptors on the postsynaptic dendrite.
- Third, the transmitter–receptor interactions may have effects that are similar or different (e.g., excitatory and/or inhibitory); thus, some synaptic events may increase the activation of the next neuron, whereas other synaptic events may, at the same time, decrease the activation of the next neuron.
- Fourth, the interaction of different released neurochemicals in the same synapse may determine their ultimate consequences in the synapse and on the dendrites.

Now let's consider processes in synapses that are related to psychology and behavior. First, a recap: Neurotransmitters are released into synapses, where they can interact with postsynaptic receptors. Neurotransmitters can also interact with receptors on the presynaptic neuron; one consequence of this interaction can be a decrease in the release of neurotransmitter from that neuron. Neurotransmitters can also be transported back into the neuron that has just released it; this process, which is sometimes referred to as *uptake* or *reuptake* or *presynaptic transport*, facilitates the reutilization of released neurotransmitter. Enhancing or diminishing these processes creates a consequence at the level of the synapse. For example, if we diminish the presynaptic uptake of an already released neurotransmitter, more than the usual amount of neurotransmitter can then remain in the synapse, extending the potential for the neurotransmitter to interact with postsynaptic receptors.

But who cares about processes at the level of the synapse when the ultimate task is to free the client from the burden of his or her symptoms? Well, just look at the transmitter–receptor interaction in the synapses: Numerous drugs that alter the uptake process, such as fluoxetine (Prozac), which inhibits the uptake of the neurotransmitter serotonin, can have antidepressant properties (see Chapter 9). Other drugs that interfere with the transmitter–receptor interaction in synapses, such as chlorpromazine or haloperidol, can have antischizophrenic properties (see Chapter 15). Synaptic processes *do* matter for psychology and behavior.

James, who has schizophrenia, holds fast to the delusion that he is visiting from another planet. In addition, his emotional responses to nearly any provocation appear to be blunted, and he is reluctant to leave his room, occasionally spending the entire day in his bed. His delusional behavior may diminish following a drug therapy (e.g., chlorpromazine) that selectively blocks one particular subtype of receptor (D2) for the neurotransmitter dopamine, even though his other symptoms of schizophrenia may remain. This is a simple example of how a specific category of symptom may be linked to a specific category of synaptic receptor in the brain of some schizophrenics.

The alteration of synaptic processes can be achieved with drugs that bind to subtypes of synaptic receptors and either activate those receptors or prevent them from being activated. For example, a receptor *agonist* drug shares the ability with the endogenous neurotransmitter of binding to and activating one or more subtypes of receptors for that neurotransmitter (Figure 6.3). In contrast, a receptor *antagonist* drug can bind to one or more subtypes of receptors, but the antagonist drug will not activate

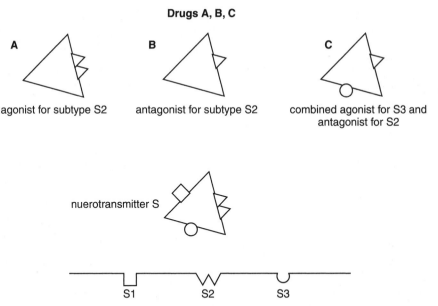

Figure 6.3 Schematic drawing of a molecule of neurotransmitter S, capable of binding to and activating three subtypes of receptors—S1, S2, and S3—in the membrane of the postsynaptic dendrite. In the upper portion of the figure are molecules for three drugs having different molecular structures: Drug A is an agonist for the S2 subtype of receptor; it will bind to and activate the receptor. Drug B is an antagonist for the S2 receptor; it will bind to the receptor and occupy it, but not activate it. Drug C has combined properties: It is an agonist for receptor subtype S3 and antagonist for subtype S2.

the receptor. By virtue of binding to and not activating the receptor, the antagonist drug is preventing the endogenous neurotransmitter from binding to and activating the receptor. Moreover, some drugs may have mixed effects upon subtypes of receptors—for example, acting as an agonist for one subtype of receptor while, at the same time, acting as an antagonist for another subtype of receptor. In summary, agonist and antagonist drugs mimic or prevent the effects of an endogenous neurotransmitter in activating synaptic processes.

Excitatory or Inhibitory Synaptic Events

Now we know that (1) neurotransmitter–receptor interactions in a synapse can be excitatory or inhibitory, and (2) the excitatory events increase the likelihood that a postsynaptic neuron will have its action potential, whereas the inhibitory events decrease that likelihood. Well, what makes the consequence of a transmitter–receptor interaction become *excitatory* or *inhibitory*? To answer this question, we need a few more details (that are important but not absolutely necessary for everyone to learn) regarding the chemical aspects of neurotransmission. Neurons (and other cells) contain fluid (intracellular fluid) and are surrounded by fluid (extracellular fluid), and these fluids contain chemicals such as sodium, potassium, and chloride. These chemicals in solution have electrical properties, because they have positive or negative charges associated with them (sodium, Na+; potassium, K+; chloride, Cl-). Because the biological properties of neurons keep unequal concentrations of these sodium, potassium, and chloride ions inside versus outside, there is an unequal distribution of positive and negative charge inside versus outside of each neuron. This inequality in the distribution of these electrically charged ions presents an instability of a sort, such that these ions have a tendency to move from the outside to the inside, and from the inside to the outside. A positively charged ion moving from the outside to the inside of the membrane of a dendrite is defined as an excitatory event, because the resulting change in the electrical–chemical properties of the dendrite increases the likelihood of an action potential occurring. In contrast, a negatively charged ion moving from the outside to the inside of the membrane of a dendrite, is defined as an inhibitory event, because the resulting change in the electrical–chemical properties of the dendrite decreases the likelihood of an action potential occurring. But what permits these positively and negatively charged ions to move across the membrane?

The ions move through channels that open (and close) as a consequence of the interaction between neurotransmitters and receptors. There are essentially two scenarios for this opening of channels: In one scenario a channel is immediately adjacent to a postsynaptic receptor; when a neurotransmitter binds to and activates that receptor, the channel opens, permitting the movement of one or another electrically charged ion. In the other scenario a neurotransmitter binds to a receptor, which results in one of several biochemical sequences of events within the postsynaptic neuron; completion of that sequence results in the opening of a channel on the membrane of the postsynaptic dendrite. To make a long, complicated story short, transmitter–receptor interactions open channels on membranes of dendrites, permitting movement of charged ions into and out of the dendrites of neurons. These events are excitatory to the postsynaptic neuron when positively charged ions move to the inside or when negatively charged ions move to the outside; these events are inhibitory when negatively charged ions move to the inside or when positively charged ions move to the outside. (See the annotated bibliography at the end of Part I for more on this topic.)

Dynamic Nature of Neuronal Synaptic Processes

Neuronal and synaptic processes in the brain and nervous system are malleable chemical events that change across time. The important principle here is that these processes, and to some extent the structures involved in these processes, are dynamic, not static. Let's examine a number of ways in which these processes in the brain can change.

• First, neurotransmitters are synthesized and stored in the neurons that ultimately release them into synapses. The rate of synthesis can be altered; the rate of synthesis can change naturally across time or in response to ingestion of a drug or food or as a consequence of a disease state. A change in the rate of synthesis of a neurotransmitter can have an indirect impact upon the amount of that neurotransmitter delivered into synapses.

• Second, released neurotransmitters may be removed from synapses at varying rates, thereby either shortening or extending the time those neurotransmitters have to interact with receptors in synapses. Spontaneous, drug-induced, dietary-induced, or disease-induced alterations in the uptake transport process or alterations in metabolism of neurotransmitters can diminish or enhance their availability in synapses, thereby indirectly affecting the ability of those neurotransmitters to interact with receptors in synapses.

• Third, the availability of specific subtypes of receptors can change. Spontaneous, drug-induced, or disease-induced increases or decreases in the number or density of postsynaptic receptors can directly affect the ability of a released neurotransmitter to have postsynaptic consequences. In other words, the result of the transmitter–receptor interaction will be changed if the availability of receptors for that interaction has been altered. There are documented differences between men and women in the availability of receptor subtypes for specific neurochemicals in synapses. These gender-related differences in synaptic processes may help to explain differences in the incidences (men vs. women) of neurotransmitter-related disorders (e.g., depression), and in the effectiveness of certain pharmacotherapeutic treatments (e.g., antipsychotic drugs).

• Fourth, a change in one synaptic process may induce a change in another process, which in turn has an impact upon the effectiveness of the synaptic transmitter–receptor interaction. For example, a drug-induced (or disease-induced) overproduction of a neurotransmitter may lead to a chronic excess of that neurotransmitter in synapses, which in turn may induce a chronic decrease in the number or density of postsynaptic receptors. This chronic decrease in receptor availability may decrease the sensitivity of that group of postsynaptic receptors to released neurotransmitter or to injected or ingested drug and may represent the underlying neurochemical basis for behavioral symptoms of a psychological disorder.

• Finally, in addition to the evidence that dynamic synaptic processes are involved in the expression of both normal and dysfunctional behaviors, there is accumulating evidence that they are vulnerable to manipulation by therapeutic approaches (including psychotherapy, drugs, and placebo) that can improve symptoms of behavioral and psychological disorders.

These examples of the dynamic nature of neuronal and synaptic processes are not offered merely for academic purposes. They can play roles in the development or in the treatment of psychological and behavioral disorders (as you will read a bit later). Moreover, I include them to reinforce the idea that the brain, nervous system, and physiology are unlike the fixed-in-time, two-dimensional figures used to illustrate them on the printed page. These chemical processes change across time, and they do not change in isolation from one another; they are related functionally and are sometimes dependent upon one another. When one of them is changed, the change is likely to have consequences for other related processes. Moreover, some of these processes are dependent upon structures that change in their number, density, or availability. For example, the receptor subtype is not a notch or a precisely shaped hole in the membrane of a dendrite, as it appears to be in our schematic representation. The receptor subtype is a three-dimensional configuration, a chemical structure embedded in the membrane. The receptor's configuration can change as its "chemistry" changes.

Perspective

Neurons release neurotransmitters that interact with receptors in synapses to communicate information to other neurons in the brain and to neurons in the sensory and motor components of the somatic and autonomic aspects of the peripheral nervous system. These synaptic processes present a focal point for understanding how the brain and nervous system integrate information to organize behaviors and psychological processes; they are themselves vulnerable to changing spontaneously across time or to disease-, diet-, or drug-induced alterations. Moreover, disordered synaptic processes can be the basis for some dysfunctional behaviors, and some therapeutic interventions can alter synaptic processes to reduce symptoms of psychopathology. In short, synaptic neurochemistry is complex and malleable, as is the relation between brain and behavior.

Despite the dynamic and complex nature of the brain and nervous system, and despite our relative ignorance of all that can be found in the brain and our abundant ignorance of how it all functions, the brain is vulnerable to scientific investigation. Various research strategies that attempt to reveal structural–functional relations between the brain and psychological processes have demonstrated their utility in improving our ability to deliver therapies for psychological disorders. Next let's look at how the brain can be studied to learn about its behavioral functions.

7

Discovering the Relation between
Brain and Behavior

How can we be certain that systems of neurons and neurochemicals in the brain and peripheral nervous system coordinate psychological processes and behavior? Imagining how they function won't tell us, but formulating hypotheses that are testable through scientific investigation is a step toward certainty. We have come to know what we do largely from systematic experimental inquiry examining the relation between the brain and behavior in humans and animals.

Strategies for Studying the Relation between Brain and Behavior

Four approaches have been used to sort out how specific areas and chemicals in the brain and nervous system are important for behavior. These approaches include lesion, stimulation, recording, and pharmacological strategies (Figure 7.1).

The Lesion Method

The lesion method is simple in its rationale: Damage (i.e., create a lesion) a specific part of the brain or nervous system and measure how behavior is changed as a consequence of the damage produced. It would be unethical, of course, for a scientist to intentionally damage a brain in a human. But human brains do become damaged as a consequence of natural accidents such as death of brain tissue due to cerebral hemorrhage (stroke), growth of a tumor or surgery to remove a tumor, repair accidentally inflicted wounds, etc. Although these accidents of nature are not conducted systematically, they do provide information about the functions of the specific areas of the brain that are damaged. It is assumed that the functional loss that follows an accidentally inflicted lesion reveals the role of that damaged part of the brain. This type of non systematic inquiry has an analogous systematic approach that can be conducted in animals (usually rats) specifically bred for scientific experimentation. Using animals, a lesion is produced in a specific region of the brain, a first step in the study of the function of that region. Damage resulting in a nonspecific lesion—all tissue at the lesion site is destroyed—can be created by administering a small pulse of electric current. Or specific damage can be created by using a drug that destroys only those neurons that use a specific neurotransmitter (Figure 7.1). If elimination of the function of a structure by damaging it can be a useful approach to learn about a structural–functional relation, might not *activation* of a function, by artificially stimulating it, also be a useful strategy?

The Stimulation Method

There are various methods by which a particular region of a brain might be stimulated or hyper-activated, including electrical or chemical (e.g., a receptor agonist drug) stimulation (Figure 7.1). Generally this approach is used in research with animals as subjects (usually rats again) because it too requires direct intervention in the brain. A stimulation strategy is essentially complementary to the lesion strategy for the study of structure–function relations. For example, if a lesion to a specific region of the brain diminishes a function, and if (in a separate experiment) stimulation of that same region enhances that same function, then these findings produce complementary, supportive evidence that the specific region of the brain is important for that function.

The Recording Method

A third strategy is less directly manipulative of the brain than lesioning or stimulating brain tissue; the recording approach encompasses a wide variety of techniques for monitoring the activity of brain in awake, behaving subjects—humans or animals. These recording techniques range from monitoring the activity of single neurons to monitoring the activity of many thousands of neurons (e.g., electroencephalogram or EEG; neuroimaging techniques). The recording approach provides correlations (Figure 7.1) between behaviors and changes in activity in specific regions

Discovering the Relation between Brain and Behavior

Strategy	Manipulation	Result	Interpretation
Lesion	Damage all tissue in area A	Behavior X diminished	Area A necessary for normal behavior X
	Destroy specific neurotransmitter in area A	Behavior X diminished	Neurotransmitter in Area A necessary for normal behavior X
Stimulation	Electrial activation of all tissue in Area A	Behavior X enhanced	Activation of area A increases behavior X
Recording	Record from multiple neurons in Area A	Brain activity increases as behavior X increases	Activity of area A correlated with behavior X
	Microdialysis sample of specific neuro-transmitter in area A	Neurotransmitter release increases as behavior X increases	Neurotransmitter release in Area A correlated with behavior X
Pharmacology	Inject agonist for receptors in area A	Behavior X enhanced	Specific receptors for specific neurotrans-mitters in area A control behavior X
	Inject antagonist for receptors in area A	Behavior X diminshed	Activation of specific receptors by endogenous neuro-transmitter in area A necessary for behavior X

Figure 7.1 Summary of theoretical set of experiments using different strategies for studying the relation between brain and behavior in animals. Note that no single result presents convincing evidence, but all of the results combined present converging evidence that a specific neurochemical in area A of the brain is important for control of behavior X.

of the brain or in specific neurochemical processes in the brain. The relatively recent invention of positron emission tomography (i.e., PET scan) was notable for providing the first technique for measuring changes in the activity of neurons in specific regions of brain in awake, behaving humans. The more recent neuroimaging techniques (e.g., magnetic resonance imaging; MRI) improve upon PET, particularly in degree of image resolution. Functional imaging techniques, such as functional magnetic resonance imaging (fMRI) and single photon emission computed tomography (SPECT), are frequently used today in attempts to map functional aspects of the human brain. These imaging techniques establish correlations between changes in neuronal activity or blood flow or metabolism in specific regions of brain and specific behaviors, psychological processes, symptoms of diagnosable psychological disorders, or behavioral effects of specific therapeutic treatments, including drug therapy and psychotherapy.

The Pharmacological Method

A fourth approach uses drugs as research tools. Drugs can be used to alter chemical processes involved in the functioning of synapses in brain (and in the peripheral nervous system). Some drugs, such as receptor agonists and antagonists, can be used to enhance or to diminish activity of neurochemical processes; other drugs can be used to create chemically induced lesions (Figure 7.1); still other drugs can be used as a component of imaging techniques that record brain activity. Imagine an experiment in which a receptor agonist drug for a specific subtype of receptor for a neurotransmitter is injected into an area of the brain, and it is discovered that the drug increases the incidence of a specific behavior. Now imagine that in a second experiment, a receptor antagonist drug for the same subtype of receptor for the same neurotransmitter is injected into the same area of brain, and it is discovered that the antagonist drug diminishes the same specific behavior. Those two findings present complementary evidence for the involvement of a specific subtype of receptor for a specific neurotransmitter in a specific area of brain for control of a behavioral process.

These four strategies for studying the relation between brain structures and behavioral functions have generally all been put to use in the study of virtually any behavior. These strategies rely on previous information regarding the locations of specific groups of neurons and specific neurochemical systems in the brain—information that is usually provided by neuroanatomists and neurochemists who conduct descriptive studies of brain structure and chemistry in animals and humans. For example, before it would be possible to accurately inject a drug that would activate specific receptors for the neurotransmitter dopamine, we would need to know the precise locations of dopamine neurons and the locations of receptors for dopamine in synapses in the brain.

So how are these various strategies put to use in a collective manner that enlightens us about the relation between brain and behavior in humans? To answer this question in a way that is interesting and exciting, let's talk about sexual behavior.

Case Study: Historical Perspective on the Brain, Sexual Orientation, and Sexual Behavior

Lesions in the brain of a rat, in the region known as the medial preoptic area, produce male rats which appear indifferent to sexually receptive female rats; these male rats with lesions appear to have lost the motivation to engage in copulatory behavior. At the time this research was conducted (the 1960s), the prevailing wisdom encouraged the consideration that the medial preoptic region was some kind of "sexual behavior center." Moreover, the prevailing assumption was that lesions to the same area of the brain in the female rat should produce female rats that lacked the motivation to engage in copulatory behavior. Instead, lesions to this region of the brains of female rats produced deficits in maternal behavior, not in the motivation to copulate. This finding was perplexing unless the researcher was willing to consider that the brains of male and female rats were organized somewhat differently and therefore functioned differently.

A short time later came the report of subtle yet quantifiable gender-related differences in the arrangements of neurons in the preoptic area of the rat brain, including differences in the density of synapses. These kinds of findings—the results of descriptive studies of neuroanatomy (and later neurochemistry)—were among the first reports that have since been followed by numerous reports of gender-related differences in the structure of the brain and nervous system and in physiological processes in both animals and humans. There are now reports of gender-related differences in (1) the size or volume of specific neuroanatomical areas of the brain; (2) the density of neurons that use a specific neurotransmitter (e.g., serotonin); and (3) the number or density of specific subtypes of receptors in brain synapses. These structural differences between male and female brains are noteworthy because they are likely to correlate with gender-related differences in the manner in which these neuronal processes function for behavior. (We'll see more on this topic as we look at specific psychological and behavioral disorders In Part III.)

Descriptions of gender-related differences in neuroanatomy and neurochemistry of the brain, together with the results of lesion studies that revealed the preoptic area of the brain to serve somewhat different functions in male and female rats, were followed by studies in which electrical or chemical stimulation of the brain could enhance motivation for copulation in male rats (and maternal behaviors in female rats). In fact, various studies using lesioning and stimulation strategies identified numerous areas of the brain (e.g., preoptic area, hypothalamus, amygdala, nucleus accumbens) and numerous neurochemicals in the brain (e.g., serotonin, dopamine, estrogen) that serve a network of neurons involved in sexual motivation and copulatory behavior in rats. Among these reports are recording demonstrations (using microdialysis probes) of the release of the neurotransmitter dopamine in an area of the brain (nucleus accumbens) well known to be involved in behaviors that are pleasurable: Release of dopamine into synapses occurs in male rats who are copulating as well as in male rats who might anticipate copulating when they are placed in the immediate vicinity of sexually receptive female rats.

Moreover, experiments using pharmacological manipulations of the brain in developing infant rats demonstrated that development of the brain during a critical period (first 5 days after birth in rats) could affect sexual "preference" during adulthood, measured behaviorally by assessing sexual receptivity to other male or female rats. These findings in rats, considered together with the reports in humans of correlations between sexual orientation (in male heterosexuals and homosexuals) and the volume of a specific area of the anterior hypothalamus in humans, raise the possibility that sexual motivation and behavior in humans is determined, at least in part, by the developmental organization of neuronal systems in the brain.

In summary, each of the four research strategies (lesion, stimulation, recording, pharmacology) have been used in experiments conducted in animals to produce information regarding how the brain organizes sexual behavior. The findings demonstrate the involvement of numerous areas of the brain, numerous neurochemicals, gender-related differences in the brain's organiziation of behavior, and evidence that processes related to the development of brain have an impact upon adult sexual behavior. Very much the same can be said for the use of these research strategies for the study of brain processes for other motivated behaviors in animals, such as eating and drinking.

Animals, the Brain, and Dysfunctional Human Processes

The use of animals as subjects in experiments to study the relation between brain and behavior is done to ultimately learn more about the relation between the brain and behavior in humans. This approach makes sense given the notable similarities between humans and animals in the structures and functions of brain. For example, humans, monkeys, rats, and even snails have the neurotransmitter serotonin (among others) in their nervous system and brain. And serotonin neurons function in fundamentally the same manner in these various species. Moreover, serotonin has been measured to have a role in the control of eating behaviors in these varied species, suggesting that the various species have some things in common regarding the relation of brain neurochemistry to behavior. So it is reasonable to claim that we can learn some things about humans from the study of the brain and behavior in animals. But can we learn about the relation of the brain and dysfunctional psychological processes by studying animals?

There have been numerous attempts to "model" human psychological and behavioral disorders in an animal species. These models do not present identical conditions in the animal as in the human, but they do provide useful strategies for studying some particular aspect of a disorder in humans. For example, an experimentally (lesion) induced hyperactive mouse is certainly not identical to a child with attention-deficit/hyperactivity disorder (ADHD). Nevertheless, if a drug (e.g., methylphenidate; Ritalin) that diminishes hyperactivity in an ADHD child also diminishes hyperactivity in the hyperactive mouse, we could conclude that the hyperactive mouse would present a useful, inexpensive way for initially evaluating the potential clinical effectiveness of a new drug to treat ADHD. If the new drug were "effective" in the mouse model for ADHD, then it may merit further consideration for use in humans. In short, the use of animals in research has proven to be a productive way in which to learn general principles about the relation between the brain and behavior, and the attempts to create animal models of human behavioral disorders have provided a vast and rich literature that has facilitated our understanding of the disordered brain and dysfunctional behavior in humans.

Among the outcomes of such research efforts in animals includes discoveries that guide the application of techniques for mapping the neuroanatomy and neurochemistry of the human brain, and the use of neuroimaging techniques (e.g., PET, fMRI) to explore possible correlations between neuronal processes in the brain and behaviors in humans.

Neuroimaging of the Human Brain

The impressive utility of neuroimaging techniques for revealing something of the relation between brain structures and behavior in humans merits further comment. The early neuroimaging technique of PET, first used in the 1970s, was notable for being the first technique for measuring changes across time in the neuronal processes of awake, behaving humans. Some of these early PET scanning devices measured the rate of utilization of glucose by cells in the brain. (Others measured blood flow to regions of brain.) This focus on glucose utilization was useful given the assumption that the most active cells would necessarily use the most fuel (i.e., glucose transported in blood); the most active neurons were then surmised to be those responsible for the behaviors that were occurring simultaneous with the PET scan measurements. For example, a person who is reading aloud during PET assessment of brain function shows higher rates of glucose utilization in visual and auditory cortical areas, and areas important for comprehension (Wernicke's area) and production (Broca's area) of speech. This approach represented a great advance in the study of the relation between the brain and behavior because until then, no techniques had approached the measurement of neuronal function across time with any impressive degree of resolution in the human brain. Within several years PET technology was improved in a manner that permitted measurement of the activity of neurons containing specific neurotransmitters (e.g., dopamine), expanding its utility.

The impressively detailed resolution of magnetic resonance imaging techniques that are in widespread use today improves upon PET. Moreover, current functional MRI (fMRI) techniques provide the ability to measure changes across time for specific neurotransmitter release, and to measure the density of specific subtypes of receptors in the synapses of awake, behaving humans. For example, combined use of MRI and PET reveals that ingestion of alcohol provokes release of dopamine in nucleus accumbens of humans. These neuroimaging techniques do have their limitations, however. The most notable is the simple fact that these techniques reveal *correlations* between activity in brain structures and behavior, so it is difficult to make inferences about what factor *causes* which effect. Determining that two events occur essentially at the same time does not permit us to conclude that one event has caused the other, nor does it permit the conclusion that it is this area of the brain only, or that neurochemical only, that is important for that behavior. In addition, these techniques require that subjects whose brains are being monitored be relatively restricted in their movements; they usually are required to recline and to severely limit their head movements. (Too few behaviors can be adequately displayed and studied when a relatively immobile person is reclining in a tube.) Nonetheless, despite these limitations, neuroimaging techniques are very useful for identifying areas of the brain that might be involved in psychological processes and behaviors. Moreover, these imaging techniques are proving to be useful in measuring changes in brain activity that appear to have been produced by psychotherapy, pharmacotherapy, or placebo.

Rudy is addicted to the psychostimulant drug methamphetamine: When an MRI is conducted on his brain, it is found to have a diminished number of dopamine receptors in a particular region. The evidence is this: A living, currently addicted person has an unusually low number of dopamine receptors in an area of his brain. The questions that remain unanswered, despite this impressive piece of correlational evidence, include:

Is this deficit in dopamine receptors the only deficit in Rudy's brain?

Was this deficit present before he became addicted, suggesting that the deficit might be considered a causal factor in the addiction?

Or is this deficit a consequence of chronic usage of the addictive drug?

Does this deficit cause the craving for methamphetamine that Rudy reports, or is it some other (unmeasured) neurochemical alteration in the brain that is responsible for his craving?

Will a therapeutic approach that reverses the abnormality in receptor number also reduce Rudy's craving or other symptoms of his addiction?

Neuroimaging techniques provide a powerful set of tools to explore the relation between neuronal and psychological processes, but overinterpretation of findings should be avoided. Because these imaging techniques are relatively new tools, we can expect to see ongoing improvements in their applicability to the study of the relation between brain structures and functions. In addition to providing information regarding the location of functional abnormalities in the brains of people who have disabling behavioral disorders, these tools will also allow us to target specific brain sites for the application of new therapeutic techniques, such as transcranial magnetic stimulation, surgical implantation of tissue (stem cells) from fetal brains, or devices for delivery of a drug into a specific site in the brain.

Perspective

Various strategies and powerful techniques for manipulating and measuring have been used to study the relation between the brain and behavior. Much of this research has been conducted in animals as a way to explore fundamental principles by which brain, nervous system, and physiology organize behavior and psychological processes. Understanding these principles allows us to use a more limited array of strategies and techniques to directly study the relation between the brain and behavior in humans. The disordered brain processes, dysfunctional behaviors, and psychopathology that seem uniquely human (e.g., schizophrenia) can be approximately modeled in animals as a way to expand our range of opportunities to use powerful techniques to study the relation between the disordered brain and dysfunctional behaviors. Despite the demonstrated utility of experimental animal models for human maladies, however, an understanding of the relation between the human brain and dysfunctional behavior will ultimately require the direct study of the human brain and behavior, including the use of techniques such as neuroimaging. As the applicability of neuroimaging techniques improves, we will gain much useful information about sites and neurochemicals in the brain that are related to dysfunctional behaviors, and about how these sites and neurochemicals are altered by psychotherapy and pharmacotherapy.

8

Principles of Pharmacology Relevant to Pharmacotherapy

Her daily use of Dexedrine (amphetamine) reduced Paula's eating well enough that she lost 60 pounds over a period of 10 months. Over that period of time her physician had to increase the daily dosage of Dexedrine twice for it to continue to suppress her appetite; she had developed a tolerance for the drug's effect upon appetite. All was fine until she began experiencing an intense paranoia that people were gossiping about her and plotting against her, and troubling, repetitive, meaningless movements of her arms (as if she were picking a piece of lint off of her sweater over and over and over and over again) began to plague her. That psychotic type of thinking and behavior was quite a price to pay for the boost in self-esteem that followed her loss of weight.

Amphetamine-induced psychosis so closely resembles schizophrenia that its symptoms are virtually indistinguishable from those of schizophrenia. This fact became known in the mid-1950s coincidentally with the discovery of the ability of chlorpromazine (Thorazine) to improve symptoms of schizophrenia. These findings together illustrate the utility of drugs for revealing knowledge about the relation between brain and behavior: The facts that the chemical amphetamine can induce psychosis and that the chemical chlorpromazine can diminish psychosis, suggest that psychotic thinking and behavior have their origin somewhere in the chemistry of the brain. It logically follows that discovering precisely *how* amphetamine and chlorpromazine alter the chemistry of neuronal processes in the brain would lead to (1) an understanding of the neurochemical causes of schizophrenia and (2) the discovery of newer, more effective drug therapy for schizophrenia.

One important general principle illustrated above is that the effectiveness of a drug in a clinical setting often provides an important step toward a better understanding of the neurochemical basis of a behavioral disorder, and this improved understanding, in turn, may facilitate development of new pharmacological therapies. This general principle is used as our starting point to consider the relation between the brain and behavior for each of the psychopathological conditions discussed in Part III of this book. Moreover, that amphetamine can induce psychosis in people using the drug to lose weight—that is, that the reduction in appetite and body weight may come at the cost of psychotic symptoms—provides an example of another fundamental principle well known to all pharmacologists: *No drug can have only one effect.*

No Drug Has Only One Effect

A drug is used therapeutically to achieve a specific outcome, the *main effect* of the drug. This main effect is the desired effect, but it is inevitable that the main effect will be accompanied by one or more side effects— effects that are not desired. Pharmacologists agree upon this important and incontrovertible principle: No drug can accomplish only the one effect that is desired; undesired effects must always be expected. Why is this so?

Consider first of all that most drugs are chemicals that are synthesized (quite literally) at a workbench located outside of the brain, nervous system, and body. A drug is therefore a substance that is foreign to the brain; it is introduced to the brain from the outside—it is *exogenous* to the brain. Because a drug is exogenous to the brain, its impact should not be expected to be a set of neatly predictable and altogether desirable outcomes; the exogenous chemical may not present a "nice fit" for the brain's own natural, *endogenous* neurochemical processes. An exogenous chemical that does not fit a specific slot within endogenous neurochemical processes is likely to imperfectly or awkwardly activate (or inactivate) a particular neurochemical process. Moreover, an exogenous chemical may simultaneously alter numerous endogenous neurochemical processes, resulting in numerous functional outcomes only one of which is actually desired. For example, amphetamine increases release, inhibits presynaptic transport (reuptake), and in larger doses also inhibits the metabolism of the neuro-transmitters dopamine and norephinephrine; the inhibition of presynaptic transport of dopamine alone may be sufficient for euphoria induced by amphetamine. As another example, the analgesic buprenorphine (Buprenex) simultaneously acts as an agonist at one subtype of endogenous opiate receptor but acts as an antagonist at another subtype of opiate receptor (Figure 6.3); this mixed agonist-antagonist property permits the morphine-like opiate analgesic effect of buprenorphine without the potent morphine-like suppression of respiration.

A drug can have multiple effects even if it alters a very specific neuro-chemical event in the brain (e.g., if it activates one subtype of receptor for one specific neurochemical). Remember that the neurochemistry of the brain is arranged in such a manner that a specific neurochemical and a specific subtype of receptor can be found in multiple areas (Figure 5.3) and therefore are likely to be involved in numerous functions or behaviors. Thus, even a somewhat chemically selective manipulation of brain chemistry may alter many different places in the brain, leading to numerous functional consequences, some of which are desired (the main effect) and some of which are not desired (side effects).

Mike's symptoms of schizophrenia could be partially improved by using haloperidol (Haldol), a drug that blocks the D2 subtype of dopamine receptors. Presumably, the relief of the delusions and hallucinations was due to the ability of haloperidol to block D2 receptors on neurons serving the cortex of the brain. But the undesired effects of haloperidol that Mike experienced—the pronounced difficulty initiating movement and the stiffness he showed when walking—were likely due to the effects of haloperidol in blocking D2 receptors serving other places in the brain, such as the basal ganglia below the cortex. Limiting the effects of haloperidol to one site and not the other would be nice, but unfortunately, it usually is not possible.

The desired and undesired effects of a drug are also related to other factors, including dosage, gender, and variability among individuals.

The Effects of a Drug Are Related to Dosage

Generally there is a relation between the dosage of a drug and the magnitude of the effect of that drug. This is true for both main effect and side effects. This relation, called the dose–response relation, can have a different character or shape depending upon the drug and the particular effect under consideration (Figure 8.1). In some cases, the magnitude of an effect may be directly related to the degree to which the drug is binding to and activating receptors in synapses—increasing the dosage may increase the receptor occupancy, thereby increasing the effect.

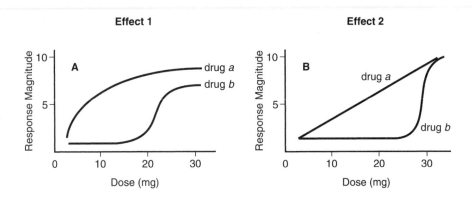

Figure 8.1 Dose–response curves for drug *a* and drug *b* for two different effects, effect 1 (panel A) and effect 2 (panel B). *For effect 1*: Drug *a* is more potent than drug *b*; greater dosages (in mg) of drug *b* are required to get an effect size comparable to that produced by drug *a*. *For effect 2*: Drug *a* and drug *b* are equally potent only when large dosages of either drug are used, and large dosages of drug *b* are required to get any of effect 2 at all.

Let's look at dosages and effects by considering the various effects of alcohol. Alcohol can have numerous effects, including euphoria, sedation, impairment of motor performance, analgesia, coma, and death. Although these effects are quite different, each is attainable with alcohol, depending upon the dosage taken. The "easiest" effect to obtain with alcohol is euphoria, because it takes a smaller dosage to induce euphoria than the dosages required to induce sedation, impairment of motor performance, analgesia, etc. In other words, some effects of a drug may show different sensitivity than other effects of a drug. For example, the smallest dosage that will produce one effect may be too small to produce another effect (in Figure 8.1 compare the two curves for "drug b" for effect 1 vs. effect 2). A pharmacologist would tell us that this is an example in which the threshold doses (i.e., the smallest dose that will produce a measurable effect) were different for two different effects of a drug (e.g., now compare panels A and B of Figure 8.2). This would be advantageous if the threshold dose for the main effect was lower (less drug would be needed) than the threshold dose for a side effect (Figure 8.2). In the case of alcohol, it is possible to experience euphoria without experiencing analgesia or coma because the threshold dose for euphoria is lower than the threshold doses for analgesia or coma. In contrast, it would be unfortunate if the situation were reversed; that is, if the threshold dose for the main effect were higher than the threshold dose for a side effect. That situation would virtually ensure that at least one side effect would precede any therapeutic benefit. To illustrate this point in relation to alcohol: If I needed to use alcohol to relieve pain (induce analgesia), I would need to use a dosage that also impaired motor performance, because the threshold dose for impaired motor performance is lower than the threshold dose for analgesia.

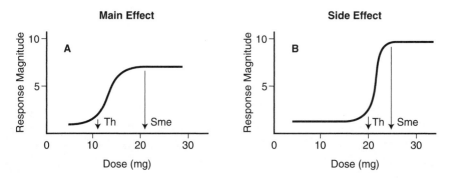

Figure 8.2 Dose–response curves for two different effects, main effect (panel A) and side effect (panel B) for a single drug. The threshold dose (Th) for the main effect is lower than the threshold dose (in mg) for the side effect. The smallest maximally effective dose (Sme) for the main effect is lower than the smallest maximally effective dose for the side effect.

Knowing the threshold dosages for the main effect and side effects of a drug is essential to achieving effective clinical treatment for at least two reasons: First, a therapist obviously would never want to prescribe a dosage that was less than threshold for the main effect. Second, knowing the threshold dose for a particularly undesirable side effect would guide the choice of dosage for safely maximizing a main effect.

Threshold dosages are not the only useful points of information that have an impact upon clinical treatment. Consider dosages that give the greatest effects: The dosage that is the smallest dosage capable of producing a maximal effect can be referred to as the *smallest maximally effective dosage* (see Figure 8.2). This dosage is useful to know for the main effect, because it would make no sense to prescribe a dosage in excess of the smallest maximally effective dosage. Doing so would only increase the likelihood of side effects without the benefit of increasing the magnitude of the main effect (compare panel A and B in Figure 8.2). In the case of alcohol, if two beers were sufficient to induce maximum euphoria, no further benefit would be obtained by drinking a third beer. (This is a fact that young users of alcohol tend to ignore!)

> Tommy's debilitating depression was relieved with a daily 20 mg dose of an antidepressant drug, but 10 mg daily was enough to induce muscular tremors for Tommy. Now that's a depressing psychopharmacological situation for Tommy, who is a neurosurgeon—the threshold dose for an unacceptable side effect was lower than the threshold dose for the desired relief of depression. What is a reasonable solution for this dilemma? Try a different antidepressant drug, or try psychotherapy instead of pharmacotherapy.

Dosages that produce effects that are in between those effects produced by the threshold dosage and the smallest maximally effective dosage can be determined from an examination of a dose–response relation for a drug's effects (Figure 8.2). This kind of information only comes from complete characterization of the relation between dosage and effect for a range of dosages from very small to very large. Comparisons of dose–response relations or curves for main effect and side effects are useful for choosing a dosage that can maximize the main effect while minimizing risks of various side effects. And that is just the trick of successful pharmacotherapy—to maximize the main effect while simultaneously minimizing the risks of various side effects. That goal is attainable on a patient-by-patient basis, when each patient's responses to dosages are considered individually, because a variety of factors that affect a drug's effectiveness vary across individuals.

The Effects of a Drug Vary Across Individuals

A drug must reach its target in the brain or body to be able to exert its effects, and there are obstacles on the way to reaching that target. Some of these obstacles are presented by digestion (if a drug is taken orally), metabolism (principally by liver), and absorption (into the blood), among others. These obstacles or processes that determine how readily or quickly a drug can get to its relevant target are sometimes referred to as the *pharmacokinetics* of the drug. The ability of a drug to exert effects is referred to as the *pharmacodynamics* of the drug. Thus, a drug's pharmacokinetics can affect the potency of a drug's pharmacodynamics.

One example of pharmacokinetics affecting a drug's effect is ingested alcohol. Alcohol can be metabolized to some degree by an enzyme (gastric alcohol dehydrogenase) in the stomach. Men have (on average) a greater amount of this enzyme than do women, meaning that women have a smaller capacity for metabolizing alcohol that is swallowed and reaches the stomach. This means that if the average man and woman (of comparable height, weight, body fat content) drink the same amount of alcohol, a greater proportion of the ingested alcohol will appear in the blood of the woman (due to the woman's lesser capacity to metabolize alcohol in the stomach). The woman is then more likely to have a higher blood alcohol level than the man, and thus essentially has a greater "dosage" of alcohol in her blood (i.e., greater *bioavailability* of the drug) available to cause effects at the various targets of alcohol. This is an example of a gender-related difference in pharmacokinetics, and it illustrates how a process that affects getting a drug to target (in this instance, metabolism) can have an impact upon the drug's magnitude of effect. Another gender-related example: In general, women require smaller dosages of antipsychotic medications than men when such drugs are used to relieve symptoms of schizophrenia.

A drug may also have difficulty reaching its target in the brain if the drug fails to cross the blood–brain barrier. The blood–brain barrier prevents some (but not all) drugs from getting out of the small capillary blood vessels and into the brain tissue served by those capillaries. This barrier protects most (but not all) of the brain from drugs that have large molecular structures, particularly if those drugs are not soluble in lipids (fats). This protective barrier can present an impediment to getting a potentially therapeutic chemical to a target in the brain where the drug can have its effect.

A variety of other factors can affect the potency of a drug in an individual, including drug interactions, drug history, and the person's age:

1. A drug's effectiveness can be altered by the current or recent presence of other drugs. For example, the use of one drug (drug *a*) may lead to tolerance to that drug, which results in tolerance to another drug that has *not* been used (drug *b*), requiring that a larger-than-usual dosage of

that drug (drug *b*) be given to attain therapeutic benefit. This situation is sometimes referred to as *cross-tolerance*. For example, a regular alcohol user may appear to be relatively less sensitive to drugs that are prescribed to diminish anxiety (e.g., Librium or Valium).

2. A drug's effectiveness may be altered by previous usage of a drug that has produced a long-lasting or permanent change in the neurochemistry of the brain, which renders the individual more or less sensitive to a drug prescribed for therapeutic purposes, or to a drug being used recreationally. For example, we could speculate that one reason a single drink of alcohol might set off a binge of alcohol drinking in a recovered alcoholic (who had been abstinent for some months) is that the person's history of alcohol consumption has altered the brain in such a way that a single dose of alcohol now has effects that it would not have had without the earlier experience of chronic consumption. That single drink may "prime" a neurochemical process in the brain, provoking a craving for more of the drug.

3. A drug's effectiveness may depend upon the age of the patient. The brain and nervous system of children and adolescents are still developing and therefore present the potential for acute (immediate, within minutes or hours) effects or long-term effects of drugs that are different from what might be observed when that same dosage of the drug is given to the fully developed adult. For example, a developing brain and nervous system chronically exposed to a drug might alter their course of development in a manner that creates a different potential in adulthood for that same drug's effects. Some statistics on addiction are consistent with this idea: Those who "experiment" with addictive drugs (e.g., nicotine, alcohol) early in life are more likely to become addicts as adults. On the other end of the age continuum, the brain and nervous system of an elderly patient may require a lower threshold dosage for a therapeutic drug to relieve symptoms of a disorder, compared to the dosage that is effective in the younger adult.

A Clinically Effective Dosage Balances Benefits and Risks

Patients present somewhat idiosyncratic characteristics and symptoms: age, one or the other gender, individual sensitivities to drugs, individual drug histories, among other differences in lifestyle, diet, attitude toward acceptable side effects, and willingness to comply with instructions for self-administration of a therapeutic drug. Given all these variables, successful pharmacotherapy is a goal that must be reached on a case-by-case basis. A side effect that is acceptable for one patient may be completely unacceptable for another patient (e.g., sexual impotence associated with a particular antidepressant). Such factors require an initial dosage that accommodates that patient's particular history, current circumstances, and expectations, including the patient's willingness to use psychotherapy in addition to pharmacotherapy or instead of pharmacotherapy. Experience with other "similar" patients may be a useful guide when choosing which drug to use and which dosage to prescribe, but ultimately success or failure of pharmacotherapy is determined by a systematic process of trial-and-error with each individual patient. Moreover, success or failure of treatment is determined by whether or not the drug improves symptoms to a sufficient degree that a patient is willing to tolerate the inevitable drug-induced side effects. In the end, a patient's compliance with the recommended drug regimen will follow a cost–benefit analysis made by an individual patient, with or without consultation with the prescribing physician.

"Grandma! Why did you stop taking your medication?"
"Because it makes my mouth dry. I don't like it."
"But your doctor told you it was important to take a full tablet, three times a day, for you to get better!"
"Yes, but I never did that. I took less. I took only half a tablet. And I only took it at night."
"But that's probably why you're still feeling bad. You're not taking enough of the drug."
"Mind your own business, child. My mouth is not dry and that's my business."

In conclusion, drugs can be useful aids for the treatment of dysfunctional behavior, but they do not provide a cure, and their successful usage comes at the inevitable cost of side effects. You will see in Part III, as we look at the pharmacotherapeutic options for treating various disorders, that there are often choices of several categories of drugs to treat a single disorder. It is sometimes difficult to say which category of drugs (or which specific drug) is the more effective for treating a specific disorder, because the measure of effectiveness for an individual patient will be made by that patient weighing risks against benefits of using a specific drug. Finally, because drugs that have therapeutic value for treating dysfunctional behaviors are reasonably assumed to act on brain chemistry (and peripheral physiology), identifying the pharmacological properties of a therapeutic drug will reveal the processes of brain chemistry that relate to behavior. The current state of thinking regarding the effects of psychoactive drugs (i.e., drugs that alter psychological processes and/or behaviors) upon brain chemistry is that psychoactive drugs usually act directly or indirectly upon neurochemical processes in synapses when altering the functioning of neurons in the brain. The synapse is the contemporary key target for pharmacological alterations of psychology and behavior.

Perspective

The use of drugs to alter the neurochemistry of the brain to relieve symptoms of psychological disorders is now commonplace. This widespread usage has provided a wealth of information, based upon examination of the pharmacological properties of therapeutic drugs, regarding the relation between a disordered brain and dysfunctional behaviors. Given this widespread usage, those entrusted with the care of patients must have a basic understanding of pharmacological principles. One of those principles—that no drug has only one effect—is of central importance for appreciating the difficulty in selecting a dosage of drug that can improve symptoms while producing side effects that are tolerable to the patient. This fact—that pharmacotherapy is not without its costs and potential for harm—encourages consideration of the use of nonpharmacological therapies together with drugs (or instead of drugs) in the treatment of psychological disorders.

Annotated Bibliography for Part II

DSM-IV-TR: Diagnostic and Statistical Manual of Mental Disorders—Fourth Edition, Text Revised. Washington, DC: American Psychiatric Association, 2000.
This manual presents the criteria that establish diagnoses of psychological disorders based upon behavioral symptoms. It is an important reference for anyone

in the business of treating or studying a person who is labeled as having a psychological disorder.

Creating Mind: How the Brain Works. Dowling, John E. New York: Norton, 1998. If you want more depth and detail on the issues I presented in Chapters 5 and 6, you should find this readable book quite interesting.

Neuron: Cell and Molecular Biology—Third Edition. Levitan, Irwin B,. & Kaczmarek, Leonard K. New York: Oxford University Press, 2002. If you enjoy reading about neurons and want to read more about cellular processes related to neurotransmission, then here is a textbook that is challenging but quite readable.

The Biochemical Basis of Neuropharmacology—Eighth Edition. Cooper, Jack R., Bloom, Floyd E., & Roth, Robert H. New York: Oxford University Press, 2003. If you enjoy reading about neurotransmission in synapses, particularly the workings of neurochemicals, receptors, and intracellular processes related to neurotransmission, then this book is worth a look. It is a challenging step beyond the level at which I have introduced you to the functioning of chemicals in synapses. It's in its eighth edition because it is the best of its kind.

Clinical Neuroanatomy and Related Neuroscience—Fourth Edition. Fitzgerald, M. J. T., & Folan-Curran, Jean. New York: W. B. Saunders, 2002. If you enjoy thinking about the arrangement of neurons in the brain and nervous system, then this is a fine neuroanatomy text for you to read. It has colored drawings, and the accompanying text emphasizes the functional aspects of the neuroanatomy (unlike many other neuroanatomy textbooks).

A Colorful Introduction to the Anatomy of the Human Brain. Pinel, John P. J., & Edwards, Maggie. Needham Heights, MA: Allyn & Bacon, 1997. This is a coloring book; the idea is to improve your ability to remember by actively tracing and coloring various portions of neuroanatomy. Some say it works.

To Know a Fly. Dethier, Vincent G. New York: McGraw-Hill, 1996. This is the very best book you could read if you want to know what a scientist is thinking when planning a research program to learn about the relation between the brain and behavior. A readable and funny book while being quite serious, the original edition was published in 1962 and yet it is timely and informative today—a classic.

Instant Pharmacology—Second Edition. Diamond, Ronald J. New York: Norton, 2002.
This is a concise introduction to the principles of pharmacology and to the various categories of drugs used to treat psychological disorders. It is readable and has much useful clinical information.

Psychopharmacology: Drugs, the Brain, and Behavior. Meyer, Jerrold S., & Quenzer, Linda F. Sunderland, MA: Sinauer Associates, 2005.
This is an excellent textbook offering a challenging introduction to the principles of pharmacology, the various categories of drugs used to treat psychological disorders, and to drugs used recreationally. Its level of presentation is a step above that in *Instant Pharmacology*.

Brain Imaging Handbook. Bremner, J. Douglas. New York: Norton, 2005.
This book is a great place to go if you would like to read more (and look at colorful pictures) about the use of neuroimaging techniques for studying psychological disorders.

DYSFUNCTIONAL BEHAVIORS AND BRAIN PROCESSES

Part III discusses behavioral disorders selected to represent a range of familiar cognitive and emotional disturbances that sometimes occur with different incidence across genders. Each behavioral disorder is explored via an emphasis on the relation between the dysfunctional behavior and processes in the human brain, largely based upon what is known from assessments of the human brain and supported by speculations about the human brain from the study of processes in the brains of animals.

9

Depression and Mania

Nothing Patty did seemed to bring her any joy. She has battled depression for at least 10 years, and in that period of time has had very little success with psychotherapeutic approaches and with antidepressant medications. The psychotherapy seemed marginally effective in getting her to understand her illness so that she had better perspective on the problem, but the general misery and malaise seemed to continue unabated. Even more frustrating, six different medications—antidepressant drugs in a variety of pharmacological categories—even when given together with psychotherapy, seemed to offer more in the way of side effects than relief of her debilitating depression. So after all of that, it did not seem so bizarre, as far as Patty was concerned, when her psychiatrist offered the option of electroconvulsive shock therapy. Her therapist predicted a 50/50 chance that the shock therapy would help Patty. She might indeed show improvement in depression following ECT, and the most likely complaint of a "side effect" would be some loss of short-term memory.

What does Patty's situation reveal to us regarding our understanding of the relation between the brain and depression? There are two points to keep in mind: First is the fact that electroconvulsive shock therapy (ECT) is offered as a legitimate treatment (usually when other treatments have failed) for persistent, debilitating depression. The second fact is that this relatively crude therapeutic maneuver—one that is not likely to selectively alter neurochemical processes or specific sites in the brain—can relieve depression with few side effects, despite this lack of selectivity. This effectiveness of ECT for relieving depression, despite its broad effects on processes in brain, is consistent with the broad variety of symptoms of depression: disturbed mood, loss (or increase) of appetite, disturbances in sleep, thoughts of suicide, difficulty concentrating, cognitive impairment, and in some cases, accompanying psychosis or anxiety. Such a variety of symptoms involving numerous behaviors and psychological processes are likely to represent a variety of underlying problems in the brain, nervous system, and physiology. In other words, it is not likely that a disorder such as depression can be understood so simply as the malfunctioning of one or two sites in the brain and one or two neurochemical systems. If multiple neurochemical processes in widespread areas of the brain need to be altered to relieve depression, then a therapeutic device such as ECT may be sufficiently well suited to the task, in part, due to its very lack of neurochemical and neuroanatomical precision. All told, these facts expose our lingering ignorance about brain processes and depression; after all, if we fully understood the neurochemical explanations for depression, there would be no occasional need for unleashing an electrical storm (i.e., ECT) in the brain as a treatment option!

The good news is that our ignorance regarding the neurochemical factors that contribute to depression is not total. We can follow the trail of relatively successful pharmacological treatments for depression to some limited understanding of brain neurochemistry and depressed mood. Before heading down that road, however, let's agree to two points:

- First, let's talk about depression as if it were a single category of debilitating mood disorder, despite knowing that it is not. Depression can be mild or severe in intensity, it can appear to be provoked by a life crisis or traumatic change (e.g., death of a loved one, loss of job, cessation of addictive drug, birth of a child), or it can occur in the apparent absence of such a crisis. Moreover, depression may appear along with symptoms of other cognitive or emotional problems; it is not unusual for someone diagnosed with depression to also show symptoms of psychosis or anxiety. But for the sake of keeping our treatment of the issues to a manageable task, let's consider depression as if it were a unitary disorder, and that the subcategories of depression (i.e., seasonal depression, atypical depression, psychotic depression, dysthymia) might have similar etiologies and similar underlying physiological or neurochemical pathologies. (We will take a similar path when considering other disorders in Chapters 10–15.)

• Second, despite our knowledge that people become depressed due to a relatively individualized, unique combination of factors, including inherited predisposition, family social dynamics, trauma, and neurochemical abnormality, let's assume that examining brain neurochemistry is a convenient point of entry to the problem—even though disordered brain neurochemistry may or may not be the most prominent contributing factor for every individual diagnosed with depression. That said, the most convenient way to learn about brain chemistry related to depression is to look at the neurochemical mechanisms by which symptoms are improved by therapeutic drugs.

Monoamine Theory for Depression

Among the earliest successful pharmacological treatments for depression were drugs in essentially three categories:

• Tricyclic antidepressants
• Monoamine oxidase inhibitors (MAOIs)
• Atypical antidepressants

Drugs in these categories have a variety of neurochemical consequences within the brain. Of note is that they all share the ability to (1) improve symptoms of depression in some (but not all) patients, and (2) increase indirectly the amount of norepinephrine in synapses (and to a lesser and variable degree, they also indirectly increase the amount of serotonin in synapses), though via different mechanisms of action. Tricyclic antidepressants inhibit the presynaptic uptake transport mechanism for norepinephrine (and sometimes serotonin), which indirectly leads to an increase of norepinephrine (and serotonin) in synapses. Monoamine oxidase inhibitors inhibit the enzymatic breakdown of norepinephrine (and serotonin), indirectly leading to an increase of norepinephrine (and serotonin) in synapses. Drugs in the third category, atypical antidepressants, also indirectly increase norepinephrine in synapses (e.g., by increasing synthesis and/or release of norepinephrine). One of these atypical antidepressants, mianserin, is also a potent antagonist of serotonin 5HT-2A receptors. This correlation—relief of symptoms and increase of norepinephrine in synapses—suggests that there is a relation between norepinephrine in the brain and depressed mood in some people. However, do not make the mistake of assuming that depression is related literally and exclusively to the "levels" of neurochemical(s) in the synapses. Remember (from Chapter 6) that the synaptic receptor subtypes permit the functions of neurochemicals in synapses.

The nature of the presumed neurochemical disorder underlying depression is not completely understood, but here are a few facts from clinical research that help to provide some rudimentary understanding about what is going on in the brain:

1. An antidepressant drug-induced chronic increase in norepinephrine in synapses causes a decrease (downregulation) in synaptic receptors for norepinephrine. This drug-induced change in brain neurochemistry occurs after approximately 2 weeks of drug therapy, which is somewhat coincident in time with the drug-induced relief of symptoms. This correlation between synaptic neurochemistry and relief of symptoms suggests that the symptoms of depression may have been caused by an increase in norepinephrine receptors (the beta subtype of receptors) in synapses somewhere in the brain. Although it is reasonable to take the next logical step to hypothesize that such an increase in norepinephrine receptors may have resulted from low levels of norepinephrine in the brain synapses, there is no convincing evidence that this is, in fact, the case or that it would contribute to the onset of depression. Keep in mind also that alterations in the amount of norepinephrine (or serotonin) in the synapses and changes in the density of receptors in the synapses would have consequences within the postsynaptic neuron: The functioning of intracellular biochemical processes would be altered (such as the synthesis of brain-derived neurotrophic factor, BDNF), and that alteration may have a role in depression.

2. An anti-depressant drug-induced chronic increase in norepinephrine (and/or serotonin) in synapses improves symptoms of depression in some, but not all, patients. This simple fact weakens the notion that depression is exclusively a norepinephrine (or exclusively a serotonin) disorder. One alternative explanation for this fact is that there may be numerous depressive disorders, only some of which are predominantly caused by disturbances in norepinephrine (or serotonin) neurotransmission. (The fact that two individuals may satisfy the same DSM behavioral criteria for depres-

sion, but only one of them responds to a drug that powerfully alters nor-epinephrine neurotransmission suggests that the DSM behavioral criteria may not sufficiently discriminate among subcategories of depression that have different underlying neurochemical causes.) Also pertinent to this issue is the fact that some subcategories of depression respond better to different drugs or to combinations of drugs that affect multiple neuro-chemical systems. For example, psychotic depression is generally more successfully treated with a combination of antipsychotic (e.g., a dopamine receptor antagonist) and antidepressant drugs. In contrast, atypical depression generally responds better to a monoamine oxidase antidepres-sant drug than to a tricyclic antidepressant drug. These kinds of findings may ultimately allow us to identify the differences in neurochemical abnormalities in the brain among the depressive syndromes that have somewhat different dysfunctional behavioral characteristics.

3. Some depressed patients who fail to improve in response to drugs that predominantly increase norepinephrine in synapses do improve on drugs that predominantly, though indirectly, increase serotonin in the synapses, such as a drug in the category of selective serotonin reuptake inhibitors (SSRIs). The first SSRI drug to be used clinically to treat depression was flu-oxetine (Prozac). The clinical effectiveness of Prozac and other SSRI drugs suggests that symptoms of depression in some people may follow too little serotonin in synapses and an overabundance of serotonin receptors, (using the same logic as used for norepinephrine). Thus a neurochemical theory for depression would hypothesize that depression may be caused by a dys-function primarily in serotonin neurotransmission, or a dysfunction in norepinephrine neurotransmission, or a combined dysfunction in sero-tonin and norepinephrine neurotransmission. The latter possibility is con-sistent with the fact that many antidepressant drugs (e.g., venlafaxine, Effexor) have a balanced, dual action upon both norepinephrine and sero-tonin synaptic processes. In addition, numerous antidepressant drugs can downregulate (decrease) 5HT-2A receptors for serotonin, whereas ECT can (seemingly paradoxically) upregulate (increase) 5HT-2A receptors. This broader serotonin plus norepinephrine hypothesis is still challenged, how-ever, by the fact that some patients diagnosed as having depression fail to respond to drugs that principally alter norepinephrine processes, and also fail to respond to drugs that principally alter serotonin processes.

Robert was not interested in psychotherapy for his depression, because it would cost money, and it would take time. And seeing a therapist might not even help. Plus, he'd heard that antidepressant drugs were generally fairly effective. But to his dismay, each of the drugs that he'd been pre-scribed in turn (one a tricyclic antidepressant, one an SSRI, one an MAO inhibitor) were only moderately helpful. But some improvement was bet-ter than no improvement, and he still rejected "seeing a shrink." So he had to choose a drug in consultation with his physician. They agreed on one of the SSRIs, Prozac. Robert preferred that particular drug not because of its effectiveness for lifting his mood, but because its side effects might be more tolerable. If he were to continue using the MAO inhibitor phenelzine, he'd have to eliminate some foods and red wine from his diet, and he just couldn't be bothered with that any longer. If he were to continue using the tricyclic drug imipramine, he'd have to put up with the side effect of ejac-ulatory failure. No way. As far as he was concerned, depression was prob-lem enough without adding to it a therapeutic drug that created another problem to really be depressed about!

In summary, there are several decades of evidence from the clinical treatment of depressed patients that norepinephrine and serotonin (two monoamine neurotransmitters) are, in some ways, involved in the expres-sion of symptoms of depression. The salient feature of this clinical evi-dence is that drugs that increase availability of norepinephrine and/or serotonin in synapses (indirectly leading to a decrease of receptors in synapses for norepinephrine and serotonin, and having effects upon the biochemistry within the postsynaptic neuron) can improve symptoms of depression in some cases. These findings nicely implicate two major neu-rotransmitter systems in disordered mood, but what exactly do these find-ings tell us regarding the brain and depression?

Drugs that improve symptoms of depression by indirectly increasing the availability of norepinephrine and/or serotonin in synapses should affect all synapses using norepinephrine or serotonin in the brain. More-over, these same drugs should also increase the availability of norepineph-rine or serotonin in synapses for neurons that are outside the brain, in the peripheral autonomic nervous system. Norepinephrine and serotonin serve multiple areas of the brain; in fact, the distribution of these neuro-transmitters in the brain is vast. A look at the maps of these neurochem-ical systems in the brain (provided by the application of neurochemical mapping techniques in brains of animals) should provide a clue to which areas of the brain may be involved in expressions of depressed mood.

Norepinephrine and Serotonin Neurons in the Brain

Norepinephrine neurons are distributed throughout the brain, serving literally each segment of the brain's hierarchy, including the spinal cord, brainstem, hypothalamus, subcortical limbic system structures, and cerebral cortex (Figure 9.1). Serotonin has a similar vast distribution serving various areas of brain (Figure 9.2). Of particular note is the fact that norepinephrine and serotonin neurons both serve structures within the limbic system—a network of subcortical and cortical structures (including the amygdala, hippocampus, thalamus, hypothalamus, orbitofrontal cortex, and cingulate cortex) that has long been implicated in behaviors in which emotion is a salient feature.

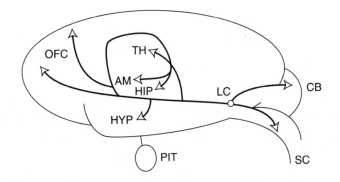

Figure 9.1 Schematic diagram of those portions of norepinephrine neurons serving areas of the brain involved in mood disorders. Norepinephrine neuron cell bodies (black dots) originate in the LC, locus coeruleus. Black lines represent many norepinephrine axons ending in axon terminals (arrows) in various areas of the brain, including OFC, orbitofrontal cortex; TH, thalamus; HIP, hippocampus; AM, amygdala; HYP, hypothalamus; CB, cerebellum; SC, spinal cord; PIT, pituitary. This drawing is a view from the side of only the left hemisphere of the brian. The structures identified are represented in each of the two hemispheres.

Knowing the locations of these norepinephrine and serotonin neurons does not entirely solve the problem of *where* in the brain neurochemical dysfunctions contribute to depressed mood. *All* of the areas served by these neurotransmitters in their synapses should show altered functioning in response to antidepressant drugs, but we can only speculate (from relatively little evidence) as to which of these norepinephrine-rich and sero-

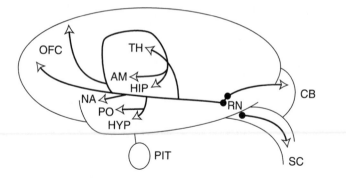

Figure 9.2 Schematic diagram of those portions of serotonin neurons serving areas of the brain involved in mood disorders. Serotonin neuron cell bodies (black dots) originate in the RN, raphe nucleus. Black lines represent many serotonin axons ending in axon terminals (arrows) in various areas of the brain, including OFC, orbitofrontal cortex; TH, thalamus; HIP, hippocampus; AM, amygdala; HYP, hypothalamus; PO, preoptic area; NA, nucleus accumbens; CB, cerebellum; SC, spinal cord; PIT, pituitary. This drawing is a view from the side of only the left hemisphere of the brian. The structures identified are represented in each of the two hemispheres.

tonin-rich areas of the brain are the more important ones for understanding dysfunctional mood. For example, it is likely that only some fraction of norepinephrine or serotonin neuronal systems need to be pharmacologically altered to relieve symptoms of depression (the main effect of the antidepressant drug). The drug-induced alteration of other (non-mood-related) norepinephrine or serotonin neurons may be irrelevant to relief of symptoms, but may be involved in drug-induced side effects.

Regarding this search for the subset of norepinephrine and serotonin neurons relevant to depression, the maps from neuroimaging technologies such as PET, SPECT, and fMRI (and shown schematically in Figures 9.1 and 9.2) have localizied norepinephrine and serotonin neurons. Recent findings from neuroimaging research have identified specific cortical (e.g., prefrontal cortex) and subcortical (e.g., amygdala, hippocampus) areas showing abnormalities in norepinephrine and/or serotonin processes in people with depression, including abnormalities in receptor number or density in synapses (Table 9.1). Some of these findings are consistent with the idea that an abnormality in number or density of norepinephrine and/or serotonin receptors in specific sites in the brain may explain some of the symptoms of depression. Whether the onset of depression is caused by abnormalities in norepinephrine and/or serotonin receptors or synaptic processes, or whether the abnormalities in norepinephrine or serotonin accompany the development of depression by

interacting with some other neurochemical (or non-neurochemical factor, e.g., stress) abnormality is unknown.

Confirmation of the importance of some of these abnormalities in the
brain for symptoms of depression comes from neuroimaging assessments
showing that some abnormalities can be corrected by tricyclic or SSRI
antidepressant pharmacotherapy that increases (compared to pre-drug
treatment neuroimaging scans) metabolism or blood flow to various areas
the of cortex (prefrontal, anterior cingulate, parietal, posterior cingulate),
thalamus, hippocampus, and striatum.

Table 9.1
Reported Abnormalities in Brains of Humans with Depression

Norepinephrine
    Fewer neurons in LC
    More alpha-2 receptors in suicide victims
    More beta receptors in suicide victims

Serotonin
    Fewer 5HT-1A receptors in cortex (FC, TC, ACC)
    Fewer 5HT-1A receptors in amygdala, hippocampus
    More 5HT-1A and 5HT-2A receptors in suicide victims
    Fewer 5HT-2A receptors in cortex (FC, TC, PC, OC)
    Fewer 5HT presynaptic transporters in cortex (FC)
    Less 5HIAA metabolite in CSF (correlated with violence/impulsiveness)

Dopamine
    Fewer D1 receptors in FC
    More D2 receptors in striatum, ACC
    Less HVA metabolite in CSF

Other
    Fewer CRF receptors in suicides
    Less CRF in CSF
    Less somatostatin in CSF
    More TRH in CSF
    Less NPY in CSF
    Abnormalities in blood flow/metabolism in PFC, amygdala, thalamus,
        striatum, caudate
    Decreased volume of cortex (OFC, PFC, ACC), basal ganglia (caudate,
        putamen) and hippocampus
    Increased volume of pituitary
    Lesions in basal ganglia

Note. There are conflicting findings for many of the abnormalities reported due to differences in methodologies used in studies in humans. Abbreviations: LC, locus coeruleus; 5HT,
serotonin; FC, frontal cortex; TC, temporal cortex; ACC, anterior cingulate cortex; PC, parietal cortex; OC, occipital cortex; CRF, corticotropin releasing factor; CSF, cerebrospinal fluid;
TRH, thyrotropin releasing hormone; NPY, neuropeptide Y; OFC, orbitofrontal cortex; PFC,
prefrontal cortex; 5HIAA, 5 hydroxyindoleacetic acid; HVA, homovanillic acid.

Other neurochemical abnormalities in depression (identified in Table 9.1) include disturbances in the functioning of the hypothalamic–pituitary axis involving abnormal functioning of the neurochemicals corticotropin releasing factor (CRF), somatostatin, and thyrotropin releasing hormone (TRH). The fact that CRF coordinates brain and peripheral nervous system responses to stress may be particularly relevant, given the potential role of environmental–social stressors as factors that contribute to the onset of depression.

Abnormality in dopamine neurotransmission might also be expected in mood disorders (Table 9.1), given the role of dopamine in behaviors that bring pleasure (see Chapter 11), and the general misery and malaise that is characteristic of depressed mood. Evidence of dopamine involvement in depression includes the fact that some antidepressant drugs (e.g., buproprion, Wellbutrin) inhibit presynaptic transport (reuptake) of dopamine, and some alter the functioning of dopamine neurons serving the nucleus accumbens—an area of the brain demonstrated to be important for pleasure. Moreover, neuroimaging studies have revealed abnormalities in the density of various subtypes of dopamine receptors in the brain during depression.

Gender Differences in the Brain

It is a fact for animals and humans that serotonin neurons, synapses, and receptors are organized differently between sexes. In humans, these gender-related differences in brain serotonin processes may be related to gender differences in the incidence of depressive disorders, which occur approximately twice as frequently in women (especially in the years between puberty and menopause) as they occur in men. Although it is tempting to speculate that the difference in incidence of depression across genders may be due to hormonal differences or to gender-related differences in neurochemical disturbances in serotonin processes (perhaps representing a relatively greater serotonin-based neurochemical vulnerability to depression in women), keep in mind that it is not likely that dysfunctional serotonin is the *only* factor in the brain contributing to the development of depression in an individual.

Indeed, the brain may not deserve exclusive credit or blame as the site of neurochemical vulnerability for disturbances in mood. Remember that antidepressant drugs should also alter norepinephrine and serotonin processes in the peripheral autonomic nervous system, in peripheral neurons that utilize norepinephrine or serotonin as neurotransmitters. Consistent with the idea that the peripheral nervous system is involved in depression are the recent findings that electrical stimulation of the vagus nerve (cranial nerve X; Figure 5.4) outside of the brain can improve symptoms of depression. It is not clear whether such electrical stimulation has therapeutic value due to its indirect effects upon norepinephrine or serotonin neurons in the brain specifically, but it is clear that neuronal processes outside of the brain are important for some aspect of mood.

Differential incidence of mood disorders between genders may also reflect differences in the way life stressors contribute to the onset of depression: In general, men appear to be more vulnerable to stress that is related to job and employment, whereas women appear more vulnerable to stress related to relationship conflict and family difficulties. Moreover, gender-related differences in vulnerability to life stressors may contribute to differential incidence in comorbidity of depression (and other disorders): In general, depressed women are more likely to show comorbid anxiety and eating disorders, whereas depressed men are more likely to show comorbid substance abuse and addiction.

In summary, gender-related differences in the incidence of depression are likely attributable to gender differences in neurochemical vulnerability *and* gender differences in the negative impact of various stressful life events. The negative impact of stress must be experienced through sensory processes of the nervous system, and the ultimate impact of stress upon the brain may be affected by gender differences in peripheral hormonal processes, but the sources of these contributing factors for depression are essentially "external" to the person.

Psychotherapeutic Alteration of the Brain

> Mom couldn't wait to have daughter Becky return home 6 months after the break-up of Becky's marriage. She missed her and was anxious to get her home to offer her the support she needed, despite the fact that Becky probably still had a number of bad habits (messy room, not cleaning up after herself in the kitchen, carelessness with the TV remote control, etc.) that required daily reminders and mini-lectures.
>
> Becky also wanted to go home but knew there would be a price to pay—namely, the unrelenting negative criticism from Mom. Becky and her therapist made a plan. Becky would continue her antidepressant drug ther-
>
> *continued*

continued

apy at home despite the fact that she currently showed little in the way of symptoms of depression. Maintenance on the drug should provide some "protection" from her mother's intensely negative criticism. Becky has also learned some coping strategies, including ways to deflect or avoid such criticism. And the therapist promised to talk to Becky's mother to instruct her regarding the potential for negative criticism increasing the likelihood of a relapse of depression.

Not only can antidepressant drug therapy alter brain processes correlated with the relief of symptoms of depression, but so too can psychotherapy. One of the better (and one of the very few) demonstrations of this is the evidence that cognitive–behavioral therapy can, while significantly improving symptoms of major depression, alter blood flow (and presumably neuronal functioning) serving several areas of the brain, including the frontal cortex and hippocampus (Figures 9.1 and 9.2). Blood flow to these same areas is also affected by the SSRI drug paroxetine (Paxil). Some of the effects of pharmacotherapy or psychotherapy upon blood flow occur in opposite directions, however.

Changes in blood flow or metabolism have also been observed when placebo has been compared to the SSRI fluoxetine (Prozac) to assess for effects upon the brain when symptoms of depression are improved: Placebo induces changes (increases or decreases) in metabolism of brain tissue in various areas of the brain, including the frontal and other regions of cortex and the thalamus. Fluoxetine produces some effects similar to those produced by placebo, but fluoxetine also alters metabolism in limbic system structures such as the hippocampus and the striatum.

These findings comparing the effects of pharmacotherapy and psychotherapy (and placebo) on symptoms of depression are interesting and important for a number of reasons:

• First, these findings illustrate that psychotherapy (or placebo) and pharmacotherapy can each affect brain processes that appear to be related to symptoms of psychopathology. This finding is important because there are precious few demonstrations that psychotherapy or placebo can affect or reorganize brain processes. By demonstrating that talk as well as drug therapy may be useful in altering disordered neurochemical processes in brain, this finding suggests that psychotherapy (or placebo) may reasonably be viewed as an alternative to drug therapy when the therapeutic goal is to reorganize disordered neurochemical processes and behavior.

• Second, psychotherapy, placebo, and pharmacotherapy can, in some instances, affect the same processes in the same areas of the brain. This finding further supports the notion that psychotherapy (or placebo) may reasonably be used as an alternative to drug therapy for targeting brain processes.

• Third, psychotherapy, placebo, and pharmacotherapy, despite affecting the same processes in the same areas of brain, can (at least in some situations) affect those processes in a *different* manner. This finding suggests that a disordered brain process may more effectively be altered by a combination of psychotherapy (or placebo) and pharmacotherapy, because talk and drug can alter the same process but they may do so in a somewhat different manner. This point is important because it may encourage the use of talk and drug therapies in combination in a manner that permits the use of a lower dosage of drug, perhaps diminishing the risk of attendant side effects. Moreover, these kinds of findings may help to explain the complementarity of psychotherapy and pharmacotherapy for the treatment of depression: For example, generally pharmacotherapy is much more effective than psychotherapy for improving disturbances in appetite and sleep in patients being treated for depression, whereas psychotherapy is more effective for rapidly ameliorating thoughts of suicide.

• Fourth, these findings (for cognitive–behavioral therapy) do not demonstrate that all psychotherapeutic strategies alter brain processes when psychotherapy is effective for improving symptoms of a behavioral disorder. Whether or not all psychotherapeutic techniques alter neuronal processes in the brain in a manner that is directly related to the relief of symptoms is an empirical question that can be answered with sustained clinical research.

What conclusions can be drawn in summarizing the highlights of what is known about the brain and depression?

• First, norepinephrine and serotonin in the brain both contribute, to some degree, to symptoms of depression in some people who are depressed. Other neurochemicals in the brain may also be involved (e.g., dopamine, corticotropin releasing factor, somatostatin, thyrotropin releasing hormone, receptors for glutamate). However, the simple fact that drugs that selectively alter norepinephrine and/or serotonin processes in the brain have impressive therapeutic value lends a great deal of weight to the notion that norepinephrine and serotonin are principal players in depressive mood disorders.

• Second, because not all people who suffer depression improve in response to drugs that alter norepinephrine or serotonin, it remains very likely that other neurotransmitters also contribute to depression in some people. It is worth noting that in comparison to the great amount of research that has considered roles for norepinephrine and serotonin in depression, relatively little has been done to assess the involvement of other neurochemicals. And don't forget all that we don't know about the involvement of neurochemicals in brain that have not yet been identified!

• Third, recent work identifying the locations in the brain of norepinephrine and serotonin abnormalities (Table 9.1) should facilitate development of new therapeutic approaches. For example, the development of drugs (or nonpharmacological manipulations such as transcranial magnetic stimulation) that can more effectively alter synaptic neurotransmission in some areas of the brain rather than other areas may provide more potent or more selective main effects with fewer side effects. Moreover, the effectiveness of psychotherapeutic (or placebo) techniques for altering neurochemical processes that are dysfunctional during depression can be assessed using neuroimaging techniques in clinical investigations.

• Fourth, it remains to be discovered which areas of the brain and which neurotransmitters, subtypes of receptors, or postsynaptic intraneuronal processes are relatively more important for the various symptoms of depression (although we could, in a moment of weakness, wildly speculate; see Table 9.2). And it remains to be determined how the various subcategories of depression are related to various neurochemical processes in the brain. Given the fact that mood disorders are variable in their behavioral appearances, it is reasonable to expect that mood disorders reflect disordered interaction among multiple neurochemical processes and neuroanatomical sites in the brain and peripheral nervous system.

Table 9.2
Symptoms of Depression, Sites, and Neurochemicals in the Brain

Symptoms	Sites	Neurochemicals
Depressed mood, sadness	Amygdala, hippocampus	Norepinephrine, serotonin
Diminished pleasure	Nucleus accumbens, thalamus	Dopamine, norepinephrine, serotonin
Worthlessness, guilt	Orbitofrontal cortex	Norepinephrine, serotonin
Appetite abnormalities	Hypothalamus, nucleus accumbens	Serotonin, norepinephrine, dopamine
Sleep abnormalities	Locus coeruleus, raphe nucleus	Norepinephrine, serotonin
Fatigue	Locus coeruleus	Norepinephrine
Difficulty concentrating	Hippocampus	Norepinephrine, serotonin
Suicidal ideation	Orbitofrontal cortex	Serotonin

Note. The associations presented in this table are the result of speculations, oversimplifications, and generalizations based upon findings in animals and humans. Keep in mind that none of the identified sites or neurochemicals functions in isolation; the sites are situated within interacting neurochemical systems.

Bipolar Disorder and the Brain

That unexpected knock on the door at 3:00 A.M. was unforgettable. "Billy, I'm here! Took the bus from Chicago. I know I should have called, but what the hell? Let's go! Got anything to eat? Put on some music! Something good, not that rap stuff. *Rap* is short for *crap*. Where's the dog? Oh, yeah, the dog died. Oops! What time do you go to church in the morning? Do you have any stamps? I've got to send some postcards. Whaaaat? No soda in the fridge?"

It was exhausting hearing it—that manic display of energy. It certainly was easier to deal with than the depression phase of the cycle, but it was three in the morning, for heaven's sake! And why did she show up here in New York? Has she resumed drinking? Was she doing cocaine again? The use of drugs always did seem to make it harder for the medication to control her bipolar disorder. Her situation seemed really out of control when she was doing drugs or drinking.

One variety of depressive disorder is bipolar disorder, what used to be called manic–depressive illness. Bipolar disorder has a greater genetic component than major depression; it is a lifelong problem that repeats with increasingly shorter intervals between cycles. Cycling between mania and depression is a double-edged problem that, oddly enough, is often treated using a single drug therapy, despite the fact that mania and depression appear to be emotional polar opposites.

Lithium carbonate, the classic chemical treatment for bipolar disorder, can successfully treat the mania, and the depression, and it can successfully prevent return of symptoms in a bipolar patient who is symptom-free. If that is not enough of a paradox, consider further that the mechanism by which lithium has these effects remains a mystery despite 50 years of successful usage. In other words, it is still not possible to confidently claim that lithium treatment improves symptoms of bipolar disorder due to effects on specific neurotransmitter processes in the brain or in the peripheral nervous system. The same can be said for other pharmacotherapeutic treatments for bipolar disorder, including the use of drugs with anticonvulsant properties (e.g., valproate or gabapentin, Neurontin) and combinations of drugs such as lithium plus carbamazepine (Tegretol), or lithium plus an antipsychotic (e.g., risperidone, Risperdal). Part of the problem here is that lithium affects so many physiological and neurotransmitter processes that it has not been possible to identify the specific mechanism(s) by which it improves symptoms.

Take this ignorance regarding the mechanism of action for lithium and combine it with the fact that lithium can be toxic (which means that careful monitoring of a patient's health is required during lithium therapy), and you see a situation not too different from the scenario in which ECT is useful in treating depression. Lithium is used to treat bipolar disorder (and mania), and ECT is used to treat depression (and also bipolar disorder), because they are effective treatments, not because their mechanism of action upon brain neurochemistry is known. The problem this presents for us is that it is not possible to benefit from our combined knowledge of lithium's effectiveness and its identified neurochemical mechanism of action in the brain to formulate a theory regarding brain processes and bipolar disorder (or mania). In contrast, it is somewhat easier to formulate neurochemical theories for depression, anxiety, and schizophrenia—theories that are based upon identifiable mechanisms of action for clinically effective drug treatments.

Despite this disadvantage, we could speculate that because bipolar disorder and depression have something in common (namely, depression), they must share some neurochemical abnormalities. we could also speculate that if it is fair to consider mania to be a swing in mood along a single continuum of emotion, but in the opposite direction as depression, then the same neurochemical processes may be dysfunctional in mania and in depression—but in opposite directions. That sounds logical, but does it constitute evidence for the precise nature of brain dysfunction in bipolar disorder or mania? No.

Evidence for abnormalities in the brain in bipolar disorder and mania can be found from recent studies using neuroimaging technology (Table 9.3). Remember that these data offer correlations between the presence of symptoms and neurochemical abnormalities; they do not necessarily offer evidence of neurochemical *causes* of the cycling mania and depression of bipolar disorder.

Table 9.3
Reported Abnormalities in Brains of Humans with Bipolar Disorder

Norepinephrine
  More (or fewer) alpha-2 receptors
  More (or fewer) beta receptors

Serotonin
  Fewer 5HT-1A receptors
  Less 5HIAA metabolite in CSF

Dopamine
  More D2 receptors in striatum (correlated with psychosis)
  Less HVA metabolite in CSF
  Less MHPG metabolite in CSF

GABA
  Less GABA in occipital cortex and in CSF

Other
  Fewer CRF receptors
  More CRF in CSF
  Less somatostatin in CSF
  Decreased volume of cortex (PFC, ACC), basal ganglia (putamen, caudate)
    and nucleus accumbens, hippocampus, amygdala

Note. There are conflicting findings for many of the abnormalities reported due to differences in methodologies used in studies in humans. Abbreviations: 5HT, serotonin; GABA, gamma-aminobutyric acid; PFC, prefrontal cortex; ACC, anterior cingulate cortex; CRF, corticotropin releasing factor; CSF, cerebrospinal fluid; 5HIAA, 5-hydroxyindoleacetic acid; HVA, homovanillic acid; MHPG, methoxy-4-hydroxyphenolglycol.

Perspective

Depression is so common that virtually each of us will have direct or indirect experience at some time in our life with one category or another of debilitating depression. These disorders of mood are variable in their etiology, duration, intensity, prognosis, and responsiveness to therapies. Despite this variability, the majority of people diagnosed with depression respond to drugs that alter norepinephrine and/or serotonin functioning in synapses of the brain, and abnormalities in areas of the brain served by norepinephrine or serotonin neurons have been identified using neuroimaging techniques. These facts implicate these two neurotransmitters as major players in the group of factors likely to contribute to the onset and maintenance of depression. This understanding represents only a beginning in the quest to know all there is to know about the relation among brain processes, peripheral nervous system, physiology, and mood disorders. Moreover, it remains unclear how neurochemical vulnerabilities in the brain interact with environmental or social stressors to contribute to the onset of mood disorders. Progress toward greater understanding of the complexity of interacting neurochemical disturbances in the brain of a person suffering from a mood disorder will require (1) refinement of diagnostic subcategories of mood disorders, (2) continued use of research to explore abnormalities in the brains of depressed individuals and the effects of pharmacotherapy and psychotherapy upon brain neurochemistry, and (3) continued exploration of gender-related differences in the brain that are involved in differential incidence of depression in women and men. A productive future for the study of brain processes related to mood disorders, holds great promise for improvement in the options for therapy.

10

Anxiety Disorders

It took Jim nearly 30 minutes to get from the family room into the car and down the driveway. That's a 2-minute trip at most, but if you need to get in and out of the car a dozen times prior to actually driving down the driveway, that 2-minute trip becomes a 30-minute one. Getting out of the car once to double-check whether the doors to the house have been locked is reasonable enough, but doing that a dozen times to check on the same door lock is a bit much. The whole process certainly slowed down his ability to get to town in a timely manner, and it was getting in the way of his having a comfortable relationship with anyone unfortunate enough to be a passenger in his car! That compulsive, ritualistic behavior was likely a symptom of obsessive–compulsive disorder, and it diminished his ability to get a day's work done.

Obsessive–compulsive disorder (OCD) is one of a number of anxiety disorders in which the anxiety or worry is out of proportion relative to the actual threat. Anxiety can be situation specific (fear of being away from home; fear of heights; debilitating, chronic anxiety continuing long after a major trauma) or somewhat generalized and nonspecific (i.e., no clearly identifiable situation elicits the anxiety). Regardless of the specific environmental factors or stressors that contribute to the anxiety, many patients show improvement in response to pharmacological treatments that alter various neurochemicals in the brain. Among the first drugs to show (in the late 1950s) effectiveness for relief of symptoms of anxiety were imipramine (Tofranil), a tricyclic antidepressant drug, and chlordiazepoxide (Librium), a benzodiazepine drug. At this point many drugs have been used successfully to treat anxiety.

Neurochemical Processes Related to Anxiety

The fact that several categories of drugs can be used to treat anxiety disorders is consistent with the fact that the subcategories of anxiety (including panic attack, agoraphobia, panic disorder, specific phobia, social phobia, OCD, posttraumatic stress disorder, acute stress disorder, and generalized anxiety disorder) are quite variable and distinguishable from one another based upon their behavioral symptoms. Therefore, it is useful to consider whether the following types of anxiety respond better to specific categories of drugs as a first step toward understanding how neuronal processes in brain contribute to anxiety:

1. OCD
2. Panic disorder
3. Social phobia
4. Posttraumatic stress disorder
5. Generalized anxiety disorder

1. OCD generally responds better to SSRIs than it does to tricyclic antidepressants (and other drugs), suggesting that endogenous serotonin has an important role to play in this disorder. Keeping in mind that serotonin neurons are widely distributed (Figure 9.2) throughout the brain (and also in the peripheral nervous system), and that SSRIs are likely to inhibit presynaptic transport of serotonin throughout the brain, it is not entirely clear *where* in the brain serotonin is dysfunctional during development of OCD or during expression of symptoms of OCD. Recent findings from neuroimaging studies, using PET measurement of the metabolism of glucose, reveal increased metabolism of glucose (and presumably increased neuronal activity) in the orbitofrontal cortex, anterior cingulate cortex, and subcortical areas, including the caudate nucleus and thalamus. This increased utilization of glucose in these areas of the brain declines following successful SSRI treatment. The utility of SSRI drugs for the treatment of OCD should not be taken to mean that OCD is exclusively due to a serotonin problem. Useful clinical effects of various other drugs implicates a variety of endogenous neurochemicals as potentially involved in this disorder, including norepinephrine, dopamine, vasopressin, oxytocin, adrenocorticotropic hormone, corticotropin-releasing factor (CRF), somatostatin, and the endogenous opioid dynorphin.

> Robin is a brilliant musician and she knows it, but it does not prevent the fear and near panic that sets in moments before each performance is to begin. Despite her complaints, Robin's physician believes that a diagnosis of social phobia or panic disorder is not appropriate, and prefers not to expose Robin to the risks of side effects associated with treatments such as tricyclics, SSRIs, or MAOIs. Instead, he recommends limited, pre-performance use of a selective norepinephrine receptor antagonist, the "beta blocker" propranolol. The medication does help Robin. In fact, the medication is a gift. She sees the crowd, she knows she is under pressure to excel. She knows it should be stressful, but she doesn't much feel stressed anymore when using propranolol—the drug seems to prevent the racing heart, the flushed face, the dizziness, the fidgeting. When using the drug, Robin plays great, and she can enjoy her performance while it is happening.

2. Symptoms of panic disorder generally respond well to treatment with one or another of the tricyclic antidepressant drugs, such as imipramine (Tofranil)—drugs that are known to inhibit presynaptic uptake of norepinephrine (and to a lesser extent, serotonin). Moreover, monoamine oxidase inhibitors, (MAOIs) drugs that inhibit metabolism of both norepinephrine and serotonin, are generally more effective for treating panic disorder (and social phobia) than other categories of anxiety. The SSRIs are also proving increasingly useful in the treatment of panic disorder and are considered by some to be more beneficial than tricyclic antidepressants, due to the fact that some of the side effects of tricyclics may be less well tolerated than those of the SSRIs. The effectiveness of benzodiazepines for treatment of anxiety that is limited to an identifiable stressor is somewhat offset by a benzodiazepine's potential for dependency when usage is prolonged. Generally speaking, when taking into account the fact that drugs in each of these categories all present their accompanying side effects, the sequence of options for attempting pharmacotherapy for panic disorder might be the following: SSRIs, then tricyclic antidepressants, then benzodiazepines, then MAOIs. The fact that benzodiazepine drugs are effective for treating panic disorder implicates the neurotransmitter gamma-aminobutyric acid (GABA) and the GABA-A subtype of receptor, because benzodiazepine drugs facilitate the activity of the GABA-A subtype of receptor. The effectiveness of benzodiazepines is consistent with findings of decreased GABA-A receptors in the hippocampus and the frontal, temporal, and occipital cortices (and decreased blood

flow to the frontal cortex) in panic disorder. So is panic disorder primarily a norepinephrine disorder, a serotonin disorder, a GABA disorder, or a disorder involving all of these neurochemicals and perhaps a few more? There is no simple neurochemical theory for panic disorder.

> "I mean I *really* hate going to parties. It's just so intimidating seeing a face I don't recognize, and thinking I'm going to have to introduce myself, make conversation, and ultimately make a fool of myself because I've said something stupid. I don't want to make new friends. It takes too much effort, it's risky, and I've already got enough friends.
>
> "The alcohol does help. The conversations are still awkward, but I worry less about it. I can deal with people better. I'm just less anxious when I drink. If I say something dumb, I just blame the tequila! But *please, do not* invite me to a party where no alcohol is served."

3. Symptoms of a social phobia, also called social anxiety disorder, generally respond more favorably to MAOIs (e.g., phenelzine, Nardil) than they do to tricyclic antidepressants, despite the fact that drugs in each of these categories affect both serotonin and norepinephrine processes. But the recent drug treatment of choice appears to be one or another SSRI drug, especially one that is effective for inhibiting reuptake of norepinephrine as well as serotonin (e.g., venlafaxine, Effexor).

4. Symptoms of posttraumatic stress disorder (PTSD) respond less well than other categories of anxiety to pharmacotherapy, but drugs that have antianxiety effects that simultaneously alter both serotonin and norepinephrine appear to be relatively more useful. And although the SSRI paroxetine (Paxil) can somewhat correct the atrophy of the hippocampus in PTSD, that finding does not entirely clarify the nature of the neurochemical abnormalities in the disorder.

5. Patients diagnosed as having generalized anxiety disorder (GAD) might first be offered a drug (e.g., venlafaxine, Effexor) that exerts a balanced, dual action on serotonin and norepinephrine reuptake processes. An alternative is buspirone (Buspar), which activates serotonin receptor subtype 5HT-1A and also blocks dopamine receptor subtype D2, thereby implicating serotonin and dopamine in generalized anxiety responses. Patients who do not respond to buspirone, would likely be offered a benzodiazepine drug; the effectiveness of benzodiazepines identifies a role for

GABA-A receptors in generalized anxiety. The ability to facilitate the activity of GABA-A receptors is a pharmacological property of alcohol. The well-known anti-anxiety properties of alcohol make it a useful "social lubricant" and a drug commonly used to diminish worry or facilitate coping with stress. The widespread availability of alcohol (no prescription needed) makes it perhaps the most ubiquitously used antianxiety drug. The addictive potential of alcohol does not lessen its utility as an antianxiety agent, considering that the benzodiazepines also have addictive potential.

Markie was prescribed a benzodiazepine (alprazolam, Xanax) to diminish the anxiety that seemed pervasive in her life. There was no problem too small for Markie to worry about. Why her husband remained unbothered by the things that made Markie anxious was not clear to her. They were both caring, dedicated parents, but only Markie would worry, really worry, that both of the children would develop sunstroke on the least bit sunny day in Syracuse, New York.

She did wish she could do without the Xanax, however, because her physician sternly warned her not to use alcohol while using a benzodiazepine drug such as Xanax—and she does like drinking socially. But she knows that mixing alcohol and benzodiazepines can inhibit respiration—she's even seen it portrayed in movies.

In summary, the subcategories of anxiety disorders are somewhat diverse in their behavioral symptoms, so it is not surprising that effective pharmacotherapeutic approaches also involve diverse categories of drugs. The list of effective pharmacotherapeutic agents consistently implicates serotonin, norepinephrine, and GABA in the brain as major players in the symptoms of anxiety, broadly speaking, although there is evidence indicating the involvement of other neurochemicals (Table 10.1). The relative effectiveness of different categories of drugs (e.g., tricyclics, SSRIs, MAOIs) for different categories of anxiety should help us develop strategies that more sharply define diagnostic subcategories of anxiety disorders. However, adequately defining subcategories of anxiety is complicated by the very high rates of comorbidity for anxiety and depressive disorders, both of which show evidence of serotonin and norepinephrine involvement. These facts preclude a tidy, unifying neurochemical theory that explains anxiety as a disorder that is distinct from depression.

Table 10.1
Subcategories of Anxiety Based upon Preferred Pharmacotherapy

Subcategory	Principal neurochemicals	Other neurochemicals
Obsessive–compulsive disorder	Serotonin	Norepinephrine dopamine, vasopressin, oxytocin, ADH, CRF, somatostatin, dynorphin
Panic disorder	Serotonin, norepinephrine	GABA
Social phobia	Serotonin, norepinephrine	
Posttraumatic stress disorder	Serotonin, norepinephrine	
Generalized anxiety	Serotonin, norepinephrine	GABA, dopamine

Note. Principal neurochemicals are those implicated by the preferred pharmacotherapy for specific subcategories of anxiety. The other neurochemicals are identified from less-preferred but useful pharmacotherapies. Abbreviations: GABA, gamma-aminobutyric acid; ADH, adrenocorticotropic hormone; CRF, corticotropin releasing factor.

Brain Sites Involved in Anxiety

Despite the lack of a satisfactory neurochemical theory for anxiety, research using animal models together with clinical research in humans has revealed important facts about various sites in the brain (Figure 10.1) and peripheral physiological processes that may be involved in the onset and maintenance of dysfunctional anxiety. Among these findings are the following:

1. Numerous regions of the human cortex seem to function abnormally in anxiety, including the frontal, temporal, and occipital cortices. Subcortical structures are also involved in anxiety, in particular, component areas of the limbic system (important for behaviors that are emotionally laden), including the amygdala and hippocampus. Some other areas showing signs of dysfunction in anxiety include the hypothalamus, thalamus, and locus coeruleus.

2. The sympathetic component of the peripheral autonomic nervous system (Figure 5.4) is involved in anxiety, in particular, for the expression of physiological changes indicative of arousal (e.g., increased heart rate, respiration, and blood pressure).

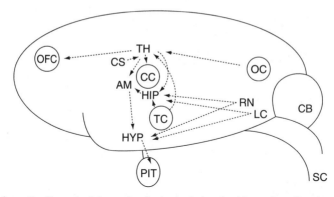

Figure 10.1 Schematic diagram of those sites in the brain involved in anxiety disorders. Labeled areas of the cerebral cortex are circled, including OFC, orbitofrontal cortex; CC, cingulate cortex; TC, temporal cortex; OC, occipital cortex. Identified subcortical areas include TH, thalamus; HIP, hippocampus; AM, amygdala; HYP, hypothalamus; CS, corpus striatum; RN, raphe nucleus; LC, locus coeruleus; PIT, pituitary; CB, cerebellum; SC, spinal cord. Lines with arrows connecting sites indicate direction of functional relationships consistent with hypotheses offered in the text. This drawing is a view from the side of only the left hemisphere of the brain. The structures identified are represented in each of the two hemispheres. Refer to Figures 9.1 and 9.2 to see the numerous structures in this drawing that are served by norepinephrine and serotonin neurons.

3. Hypotheses attempting to link brain sites (Figure 10.1) to anxiety include the following: Prolonged stress can increase the release of CRF from the hypothalamus, leading to an increase in peripheral adrenocorticotropin hormone (ACTH) and cortisol in the blood. Chronic exposure to increased cortisol diminishes the neuronal capacity of the hippocampus (it atrophies). This diminished hippocampal function is important because it is the hippocampus, the amygdala, and the cortex that receive sensory information from the thalamus, collected from sensory processes that monitor the environment (Figure 5.1). The diminished state of the hippocampus leads the amygdala to register and communicate fear that is out of proportion to the information being received from the environment through the thalamus and from cortical processes. In addition, this hippocampal–amygdala connection has diminished capacity to organize the activity of the hypothalamic–pituitary axis. The resulting abnormal hypothalamic–pituitary function, together with abnormal functioning of norepinephrine neurons originating in the locus coeruleus, results in exaggerated activity of the sympathetic component of the autonomic nervous system (Figure 5.1). Although this scenario involves numerous sites in the brain (Figure 10.1) working in concert with the peripheral

nervous system, it still is overly simplistic in terms of providing an explanation of how and why the various subcategories of anxiety dysfunctions appear.

Another simple hypothesis attempting to explain brain processes and specifically the anxiety of OCD is the following: Dysfunction of the corpus striatum (Figure 10.1) results in abnormal processing of sensory information by the thalamus, in turn leading to hyperactivity in the orbitofrontal and anterior cingulate cortices. The hyperactivity in the orbitofrontal cortex is seen as responsible for the intrusive thoughts that characterize OCD, whereas hyperactivity of the cingulate cortex is seen as responsible for the accompanying anxiety.

4. The hypotheses in the preceding point regarding brain sites and processes identify sites served by neurons utilizing a variety of neurochemicals, including serotonin, norepinephrine, dopamine, GABA, CRF (among others; see Table 10.1), each of which has been implicated in anxiety responses based upon the clinical effectiveness of therapeutic drugs.

5. Neuroimaging studies using PET, SPECT, and fMRI, applied to the brains of humans diagnosed as having one or another category of anxiety disorder, have identified abnormalities in various areas of brain (Table 10.2). These numerous abnormalities in blood flow, glucose metabolism, or synaptic receptor number do not yet permit a clear picture relating subcategories of anxiety to specific sites in the brain. Moreover, these abnormalities in numerous sites in the brain are not easily integrated into the simplistic hypotheses in point 3 above, relating sites in the brain to dysfunctional anxiety.

Gender Differences Related to Anxiety

The incidence of anxiety disorders generally is greater for women than for men, approximating a ratio of 3:2. In addition, the ratio of incidence of panic disorders is approximately 2.5:1 for women:men, generalized anxiety disorder is more common in women than men, but the incidence of OCD onset in childhood is greater for men than women. As we saw for mood disorders (Chapter 9), it is not likely that these gender differences in incidence are attributable exclusively to environmental stressors or exclusively to (as yet unidentified) gender-related differences in vulnerability for malfunctioning brain processes related to anxiety. It is notable, however, that there are gender differences in areas of the brain known to

Table 10.2
Sites in the Brain Showing Abnormalities for Subcategories of Anxiety

Sites	Subcategories of Anxiety Disorders					
	OCD	Panic	Social Phobia	PTSD	Social	GAD
Cortical:						
Orbitofrontal	x—a			x		
Medial prefrontal	x	x—b		x—b	x—c	x
Temporal prefrontal				x		
Dorsolateral prefrontal				x	x—c	
Inferior frontal	x					
Temporal	x	x—b	x	x		x
Parietal	x			x		
Occipital (visual)		x—b				x
Visual association			x	x		
Somatosensory			x			
Somatomotor				x		
Anterior cingulate	x—a	x				
Posterior cingulate			x	x		
Parahippocampal gyrus			x—c		x—c	
Insula	x					
Caudate	x—a					x
Amygdala				x	x—c	
Hippocampus		x—b	x	x—a	x—c	
Thalamus	x—a		x	x		
Cerebellum				x		

Note. An x identifies sites in the brain showing abnormalities in blood flow, glucose metabolism, or receptor number as identified by PET, SPECT, or fMRI neuroimaging assessment. Abbreviations: OCD, obsessive–compulsive disorder; PTSD, posttraumatic stress disorder; GAD, generalized anxiety disorder; a, normalized by SSRI pharmacotherapy; b, fewer GABA-A receptors; c, normalized by cognitive–behavioral therapy.

be dysfunctional in anxiety disorders, including the hippocampus, hypothalamus, and cortex, and also number and density of receptors serotonin neurons and receptors. Moreover, the involvement of serotonin in depression and the high rates (> 50%) of comorbidity of anxiety and depression raise the possibility that gender-related differences in anxiety and depression may share neurochemical mechanisms as factors contributing to the psychopathology.

Effects of Psychotherapy upon the Brain

Very little is known about effects of psychotherapy upon the brain in the treatment of anxiety disorders. It is known, in patients whose symptoms of OCD have been improved by cognitive–behavioral therapy, that there is a decrease of glucose metabolism (and presumably neuronal functioning) in the orbitofrontal cortex, caudate nucleus, and thalamus, as determined using PET neuroimaging. This metabolic–neuronal change can also be induced by SSRI pharmacotherapy, indicating that pharmacotherapy or psychotherapy can produce similar changes in the same areas of the brain in the treatment of OCD (Table 10.2). A second example concerns the effects of an SSRI drug and the effects of cognitive–behavioral therapy upon social phobia: Pharmacotherapy or psychotherapy produces similar changes in blood flow to the amygdala, hippocampus and surrounding cortical and subcortical areas of the brain as symptoms improve. Another example is that cognitive-behavioral therapy for a specific phobia (e.g., heights, spiders) can "normalize" abnormalities in blood flow to the dorsolateral prefrontal cortex and the parahippocampal gyrus (i.e., the cortex surrounding the hippocampus).

These kinds of findings do not necessarily mean that psychotherapy and pharmacotherapy exert their effects upon symptoms of OCD, social phobia, or specific phobia through identical neurochemical mechanisms at those specific neuroanatomical sites, but they do raise interesting issues (as discussed in detail in Chapter 9) concerning the combined or separate usage of psychotherapy and pharmacotherapy.

Understanding the effects of psychotherapy and pharmacotherapy on brain processes is particularly pertinent for the treatment of anxiety disorders for several reasons: First, the fact that not all symptoms of anxiety disorders respond particularly well to pharmacotherapy alone demands a consideration of using psychotherapy as an adjunct. Second, the sequential use of different therapeutic approaches is sometimes of benefit in treating anxiety. For example, cognitive–behavioral therapy is often begun prior to the initiation of pharmacotherapy for the treatment of panic disorder. The use of psychotherapy prior to the initiation of drug therapy may be particularly important in cases where the latency for drug-induced benefit is rather long (e.g., benzodiazepines have a shorter latency to improve symptoms of anxiety than do tricyclics or SSRIs). Third, psychotherapy could be used solely when research indicated equal effects with pharmacotherapy on brain processes, thereby avoiding medication side effects. If it could be demonstrated that a psychotherapeutic-induced change mediated by GABA, for example, could substitute for a pharmacotherapeutic-induced change in GABA for long-term maintenance therapy for anxiety (e.g., in posttraumatic stress disorder), the patient would then not need to be exposed chronically to the addictive properties (and other side effects) of a benzodiazepine (GABA agonist) drug.

Perspective

The multiple diagnostic subcategories of anxiety reflect its varied behavioral forms. The symptoms of anxiety in these various diagnostic subcategories appear to be related to numerous neurochemical processes and sites in the brain—so numerous and overlapping across subcategories of anxiety that no satisfactory neurochemical theory of anxiety exists yet. Complicating this situation further is the fact that anxiety and depression may represent manifestations of common neurochemical vulnerabilities, particularly for serotonin and norepinephrine. Consistent with this idea are four facts: First, symptoms of depression and anxiety often coexist whether the ultimate diagnosis is depression or anxiety. Second, many of the drugs (e.g., SSRIs) and a number of the psychotherapeutic techniques (e.g., cognitive–behavioral therapy) used successfully to treat anxiety are also used successfully to treat depression. Third, many of the same areas of the brain are dysfunctional in both anxiety and depression. Fourth, many of the same life stressors may contribute to either anxiety or depression. Achieving greater clarity regarding the relation among brain sites, brain neurochemicals, social–environmental stressors, and symptoms of anxiety disorders will require (1) reassessment of the way behavioral symptoms are used to establish criteria for defining categories of anxiety disorders and mood disorders; and (2) continued use of neuroimaging strategies to assess neurochemical abnormalities throughout the brain in people suffering from anxiety disorders; and (3) neuroimaging strategies to assess the impact of psychotherapy and pharmacotherapy upon neurochemical processes related to anxiety.

11

Substance Use Disorders

A drug has immediate, acute consequences upon the brain and body. When these consequences are perceived by the user as pleasurable (e.g., inducing a feeling of euphoria), the likelihood that the drug will be used again increases, despite the fact that the same drug may also produce negative consequences. The repeated use of a drug can induce changes in the brain that may result in chronic use (addiction/dependence) and occasional abuse (maladaptive use) of a drug. What is going on in the brain during disorders of drug usage?

One way to begin to address this question is to examine the acute versus long-term consequences of the use of specific drugs upon neurochemical processes in the brain. This examination has been conducted in research using animals and humans, leading to a great deal of knowledge about the neurochemical consequences of drug ingestion.

Effects of Drugs upon Brain Neurochemistry

Drugs used recreationally (i.e., in order to have "fun") include substances in a variety of pharmacological categories. Let's first look at a sampling of these drugs with a limited focus upon their acute effects on the neurochemistry of the brain:

1. Alcohol, perhaps the most widely used recreational drug, has a variety of nonspecific effects upon tissues and cellular and neuronal processes. Alcohol also has some acute effects upon specific neurochemicals. For example, alcohol inhibits synaptic activity of the neurotransmitter glutamate by diminishing the ability of glutamate to bind to the synaptic

N-methyl-D-aspartate (NMDA) subtype of receptors. In addition, alcohol directly facilitates the activity of the GABA-A subtype of receptor for the neurotransmitter GABA, which is widely distributed throughout the brain. It is the enhancement of GABA neurotransmission that is likely to explain antianxiety properties of alcohol, but the ability of small amounts of alcohol to induce euphoria may be due to the indirect effect of alcohol to enhance the functioning of neurons that release dopamine in the nucleus accumbens of the brain.

2. Nicotine, one of the most powerfully addictive substances, directly activates the nicotinic subtype of receptors for the neurotransmitter acetylcholine (ACh). ACh neurons are more limited in their distribution in the brain than are norepinephrine, dopamine, or serotonin neurons, but some ACh neurons send their axons to synapses in the nucleus accumbens of the brain. This particular neuronal connection explains the ability of nicotine to indirectly enhance the functioning of dopamine neurons in the nucleus accumbens.

3. Marijuana, a plant that is readily available despite it being illegal to use, contains delta-9-tetrahydrocannibinol (THC), which can activate several subtypes of cannabinoid receptors in the synapses of the brain. In addition, THC can indirectly provoke the release of dopamine from neurons serving the nucleus accumbens.

4. Heroin, another powerfully addictive substance, is converted into morphine in the brain to activate multiple subtypes of synaptic receptors for endogenous opiate neurochemicals. This activation of opiate receptors explains the ability of heroin to indirectly provoke the release of dopamine from neurons serving the nucleus accumbens.

5. Amphetamine, methamphetamine, and cocaine have multiple effects upon neurotransmission for at least three endogenous neurochemicals: dopamine, norepinephrine, and serotonin. Among these various effects, these drugs can enhance the release of dopamine and inhibit the presynaptic uptake transport process for dopamine throughout the brain, including dopamine in the nucleus accumbens.

> Alan enjoyed the effects of alcohol, especially the light euphoria that followed that first glass of champagne, or the second beer. He also enjoyed the distortion of time, the heavy, relaxed feeling that he had when smoking a joint. He even liked its sweet smell, but he always successfully avoided the
> *continued*

continued
paranoia that he twice experienced when smoking too much of some really potent grass. He snorted cocaine once and did not like it—it was too big
a wallop, too fast. He did not like that sense of losing control. He had not
tried "harder" drugs such as heroin. He did not want to begin to think of
himself as a junkie, and he could do without others thinking of him as some
kind of hooplehead.

Recently he'd noticed a change in his attitude toward his recreational
use of drugs. Before, just about 2 years ago, he was reluctant to use anything but alcohol and marijuana. Now, when offered something new—
something potentially more exciting—he seemed attracted by the
opportunity. It was almost as if his brain had been "primed" to be ready
for newer, more exciting pharmacological challenges. That new perspective did worry him. It almost seemed as if his early use of the tamer substances had been an investment in bigger, scarier things to come.

There are both differences and similarities among the drugs we just considered. Alcohol is usually listed as being a central nervous system depres-
sant or a sedative/hypnotic category of drug. Nicotine is listed as a
psychomotor stimulant, as are amphetamine, methamphetamine, and
cocaine. Heroin is classified as an opiate analgesic. Marijuana is usually
classified as a so-called psychedelic substance. These drugs have rather distinctly different effects upon psychological processes and behavior, but
they also have three important points in common: First, consumers of
these drugs report pleasure associated with the usage of the drug. Second,
each of these drugs can be found to be used chronically: We know about
alcoholism and addictions to nicotine, heroin, cocaine, and methamphetamine, and we know of daily users of marijuana. Third, these different
drugs, despite their different psychoactive properties and their different
acute effects upon the neurochemistry of the brain, all increase dopamine
neurotransmission in the brain. Is it a mere coincidence that so many drugs
used habitually for their pleasurable consequences also have effects upon
dopamine neurotransmission? Or is there an important relation among
dopamine in the brain, the experience of pleasure and a person's chronic
usage? What do we know about pleasure and processes in the brain?

The brain has at least one system of neurons that serves the psychological process of pleasure. The earliest hypothesis of a "pleasure center" in
the brain appeared in the mid-1950s to explain the finding that laborato-
ry rats could be taught to perform work (e.g., press a lever in their cage)

to activate the delivery of mild electrical stimulation (Figure 2.4) to a specific region of the brain: the hypothalamus. These experiments demonstrated that passing very small amounts of electric current through electrodes that were surgically implanted in the hypothalamus seemed to have reward value; that is, the rat found this "self-stimulation" experience pleasurable and would do work to obtain it. A reasonable interpretation at the time was that the hypothalamus was a "pleasure center" of some sort—a group of neurons activated by behaviors having pleasurable consequences.

Dopamine Neurons and Pleasure

Investigations in animals of this self-stimulation phenomenon revealed not a circumscribed pleasure center but the involvement of many neurons serving wide regions of the brain, including neurons in the ventral tegmental area (VTA) that release dopamine into synapses of the nucleus accumbens, which lies forward of the hypothalamus (Figure 11.1). This self-stimulation phenomenon is not unique to rats; it has been demonstrated in at least 20 species, including humans. Some of this research in the relation between brain neurochemistry and pleasure uses microdialysis recording techniques (Figure 2.4) in animals and neuroimaging techniques in humans. These strategies can be used in ways that permit the measurement of dopamine neurotransmission in synapses. Increased dopamine neurotransmission in the nucleus accumbens accompanies behaviors such as the following: eating sweet or fatty foods, usage of amphetamine, cocaine, nicotine, or THC, ingestion of alcohol, copulation, or listening to one's preferred music.

> Nothing compared to the pleasure of playing music in front of a crowd of people who were dancing, showing their interest, and sometimes screaming out their delight. It was the one thing that kept Marty motivated, helped him focus his energy to keep working at the development of his technical abilities as a rock musician. But those long stretches of not performing live were a problem for him. It was like he'd lost his "drug" when the band was off the performance tours. He needed—no, he *craved*—a suitable substitute. The only thing that seemed like a suitable substitute was having sex, or maybe cocaine. And the cocaine was often the more attractive of the two—he didn't need to work at an intimate relationship to get his fix from the drug!

A wide variety of behaviors that have in common the ability to bring one type of pleasure or another also share the ability to directly or indirectly activate dopamine neurons to release dopamine into synapses of the nucleus accumbens. This fact does not make the nucleus accumbens the brain's "pleasure center," nor does it make dopamine the brain's "pleasure chemical," but it does reveal that the nucleus accumbens–dopamine connection is one aspect of the brain that has a very important role to play in our experience of pleasure. Pleasure can be induced by drugs that directly enhance the functioning of dopamine synapses in the nucleus accumbens (e.g., methamphetamine, cocaine) and by drugs that act upon opiate receptors (e.g., heroin, morphine; the painkiller oxycodone [Oxycontin is one brand name]) in the VTA, thereby enhancing the functioning of VTA dopamine neurons that have axons projecting to the nucleus accumbens and other areas of the brain (Figure 11.1).

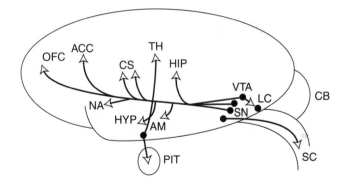

Figure 11.1 Schematic diagram of those portions of dopamine neurons serving areas of the brain involved in substance use disorders. Dopamine neuron cell bodies (black dots) originate in several areas, including the VTA, ventral tegmental area, and the SN, substantia nigra. Black lines represent dopamine axons ending in axon terminals (arrows). Abbreviations: OFC, orbitofrontal cortex; ACC, anterior cingulate cortex; TH, thalamus; HIP, hippocampus; AM, amygdala; HYP, hypothalamus; NA, nucleus accumbens; CS, corpus striatum; LC, locus coeruleus; PIT, pituitary; CB, cerebellum; SC, spinal cord. This drawing is a view from the side of only the left hemisphere of the brain. The structures identified are represented in each of the two hemispheres.

What does it mean that so many different drugs, many of them having addictive potential, share an ability with tasty food, great music, and an attractive mate to increase the release of dopamine in the nucleus accumbens? The findings that recreational drugs alter the identical neurochemical processes as do non-drug-taking behaviors that also have pleasurable outcomes suggest that the recreational use of drugs is an alternative and somewhat artificial way to activate the neurochemical reward processes of the brain. That does not make recreational drug usage appropriate or justifiable, but it may well explain its rather high incidence: Drugs can quickly and powerfully activate these pleasure processes in the brain. The use of drugs in this manner may provide a more robust, exhilarating experience than can other behaviors that have pleasurable consequences (with the possible exception of orgasm). If the risks associated with drug usage could be kept to a manageable "cost," drug-taking behavior might be as common as eating one's favorite foods—and might be pleasurable (as is eating) due to the same underlying brain neurochemical processes. Drug-taking behavior might also be particularly pleasurable for people suffering a mood disorder (e.g., depression), especially if the mood disorder is due to deficient neurotransmission of dopamine, serotonin, or norepinephrine. Correcting a neurochemical deficiency by using a recreational drug may represent "self-medication" for that disorder. The chronic use of a recreational drug to self-medicate for a mood disorder ultimately could lead to diagnosis of a comorbid substance use.

The Neurochemistry of Addiction/Dependence

The drug-taking behaviors observed in addicts characterize addiction (or dependence) as a chronic, relapsing disease involving brain processes. This possibility suggests that the following is true for addicts: Drug taking may be initiated voluntarily, but repeated drug ingestion reorganizes brain chemistry in a manner that can result in compulsive drug-seeking behaviors and a psychological process of craving in the addicted brain. Once craving begins, drug taking may now be somewhat less voluntary; instead it may be intensely motivated by desire for the drug-induced pleasure, and it may also be motivated by the knowledge that drug taking will prevent unpleasant feelings associated with abstinence (i.e., withdrawal symptoms). In fact, the factors that contribute to continued drug usage are numerous and include physiological, neurochemical, psychological, and social components. But let's focus for a moment on one key aspect of this large problem: What evidence supports the idea that drug usage can reorganize the brain in a manner that increases the likelihood that drug usage will become chronic? Table 11.1 summarizes the research findings in this area.

Table 11.1
Reported Abnormalities in Brains of Humans Using Psychoactive Drugs

Cocaine
    Fewer D2 dopamine receptors
    More 5HT transporters (after detoxification)
    More mu opioid receptors (correlated with craving)
    Decrease in blood flow/metabolism in cortex (ACC, OFC) (after
       detoxification)
    Increase in blood flow/metabolism in cortex (ACC, OFC) (in active users)
    Increase in blood flow/metabolism in cortex OFC (exposure to drug
       paraphernalia)

Methamphetamine
    Fewer D2 dopamine receptors
    Fewer dopamine transporters (after detoxification)
    Decrease in blood flow/metabolism in cortex (OFC), thalamus, striatum
    Increase in blood blow/metabolism in parietal cortex

Methylphenidate (Ritalin)
    Increase in blood flow/metabolism in ACC
    Increase in blood flow/metabolism in OFC (correlated with craving)

Ecstasy
    Fewer 5HT neurons
    Fewer 5HT transporters
    Decrease in blood flow/metabolism in amygdala and striatum

Nicotine
    Less MAO-A and MAO-B (in active smokers)
    Fewer D1 dopamine receptors in striatum
    Increase in blood flow/metabolism in cortex (ACC, temporal) (correlated
       with craving)

Alcohol
    Fewer benzodiazepine receptors
    Fewer dopamine transporters in striatum (normalized by abstinence)
    Fewer D2 and D3 dopamine receptors
    Fewer 5HT transporters in brainstem (in alcoholics)

Marijuana
    Decrease in blood flow/metabolism in cerebellum (during early abstinence)
    Increase in blood flow/metabolism in cortex (OFC, ACC) and cerebellum

Opiates
    Fewer D2 dopamine receptors
    Increase in blood flow/metabolism in cortex (OFC) (correlated with craving)

Note. This is not an exhaustive listing, and there are conflicting findings for many of the abnormalities reported due to differences in methodologies used in studies in humans. Abbreviations: 5HT, serotonin; PFC, prefrontal cortex; ACC, anterior cingulate cortex; MAO, monoamine oxidase.

Results from neuroimaging studies in humans demonstrate the following for cocaine users: Cocaine ingestion increases the amount of dopamine in synapses. A chronic state of excess dopamine in synapses could induce the measured downregulation (decrease) of dopamine D2 receptors in the striatum of the human brain. This downregulation is correlated with decreased utilization of glucose (and presumably decreased neuronal functioning) in the orbitofrontal cortex (Figure 11.1). These findings together support the hypothesis that cocaine-induced downregulation of D2 receptors mediates dysregulation of the orbitofrontal cortex, which creates the underlying neurochemical mechanism for compulsive drug seeking and ingestion. This hypothesis is further supported by the findings that changes in glucose metabolism in the orbitofrontal cortex are positively correlated with the reported intensity of craving for cocaine.

These findings of drug-induced altered dopamine neurotransmission are not unique to ingestion of cocaine. Chronic usage of methamphetamine, heroin, or alcohol causes (or is correlated with) downregulation of dopamine D2 receptors in the brain (Table 11.1), and this abnormality persists after drug use is terminated, suggesting that the drug-induced change in brain neurochemistry can be permanent.

> Viv had not used drugs in 2 years, and she had moved out of town to get away from the people and the places, the very sight of which would get her thinking about using again. New town, new job, new friends—but still, when sitting at home with none of the old cues around, she sometimes thought about using. They weren't really thoughts or ideas about using—they were obsessions, really. She couldn't escape them. They were now a part of her, even 2 years after she'd quit. Viv knew that she was a different person now, different inside . . . in her head.

The notion that downregulation of dopamine D2 receptors is an important part of the neurochemistry that provokes compulsive drug seeking and ingestion of a drug is consistent with the finding that some non-substance-abusing humans—those who have relatively lower D2 receptor density in the brain—report more intense pleasurable effects of the stimulant drug methylphenidate (Ritalin; a drug having amphetamine-like properties) than those whose D2 receptor density levels are "normal." Thus using drugs may represent "self-medication" for a preexisting D2 dopamine deficiency in the brain. Could it be that some proportion of substance-using and -abusing people are merely attempting to bring the dopamine neurochemistry of their brain into a more normal state?

As noted in Table 11.1, other drugs induce neurochemical changes in the brains of humans. For example, the drug known as ecstasy (MDMA) decreases glucose metabolism in the striatum and amygdala, and it can damage the presynaptic reuptake transport process for serotonin neurons. In addition, alcoholics show increased metabolic activity in the prefrontal cortex and thalamus, and there is some pathology of the frontal lobes of the cortex. Opiate users and nicotine users have downregulation of dopamine receptors, and users of THC show decreased metabolism of glucose in the cerebellum, an area where cannabinoid receptors are abundant.

In summary, various findings from research in humans (and animals) support the idea that the usage of a variety of drugs that have addictive potential alters processes related to the functioning of dopamine in the brain, which leads to disordered functioning of the orbitofrontal cortex—which, in turn, may induce the craving and compulsive drug-seeking behavior characteristic of addiction or dependence. These drug-induced changes in the brain may be long-lasting or even permanent, a finding that is consistent with the idea that addiction is a chronic, relapsing disorder of behavioral and brain processes. Furthermore, drug-induced changes may not occur exclusively in synaptic processes, but may be related to intracellular changes in postsynaptic neuronal processes (e.g., those associated with biochemical factors, such as brain-derived neurotrophic factor; BDNF).

> One day at a time. Some days were easier than others for Chrissie. The craving was a bit less intense nearly every day; that was probably because of the prescription drug. But there were some days that were tougher than others—the days when Billy stopped by, or when she bumped into Billy somewhere in town. It just seemed like Billy was a stimulus to think about drinking again. The therapist had advised her not to see Billy, but she couldn't bring herself to ask Billy to just disappear from her life altogether. It was *her* problem, not Billy's. All in all, things seemed to be working so long as she took the medication regularly, as well as the advice she had been offered about restructuring her life—from the bottles in her cabinets to her social calendar. It worked so long as Chrissie kept her focus. One day at a time.

Treatment of Addiction/Dependence

Addiction is a chronic, relapsing disorder of behavioral and brain process-es exhibited by individuals living in specific social contexts. Despite the fact that drug ingestion appears to alter the brain in ways that result in compulsive usage, it is not likely that treatments that only alter brain processes will solve the problem of chronic drug ingestion that occurs in social contexts. Moreover, the difficulty of treating drug users is made more complicated by the fact that so many (approximately 80%) of indi-viduals who satisfy DSM criteria for substance dependence or substance abuse disorders also are likely to meet criteria for one or another psychi-atric disorder (including mood and anxiety disorders).

Treatment programs for addiction/dependence generally attack the problem in two parts: First, abstinence from drug taking must be accom-plished. Second, once abstinence is initiated, steps to diminish the likeli-hood of resuming drug usage need to be put into place.

How do therapeutic approaches for substance use affect the brain and behavior? Pharmacotherapeutic approaches attempt to prevent or reverse the acute or long-term effects of the abused drug upon the brain by capi-talizing upon what is known about effects of the ingestion of the abused drug upon brain processes. Psychotherapeutic techniques for treatment of substance use generally take a different angle of approach.

Pharmacotherapy for Addiction

Pharmacotherapeutic approaches have been used to address the two important goals in treating addiction: initiating abstinence or detoxifica-tion and delaying or preventing resumption of usage. Let's look at a few examples of pharmacotherapy, focusing on the impact of therapeutic drugs upon processes in the brain.

The facilitation of abstinence can be achieved by substituting a "thera-peutic" drug for the "abused" drug; the goal is to support abstinence while minimizing the negative consequences of withdrawal symptoms. For example, the drug benzodiazepine can be used as pharmacotherapy for the alcoholic, who can then begin detoxification by completely stopping the use of alcohol. This step is followed by weaning off the benzodi-azepine therapy as the treatment program continues. This approach cap-italizes on the fact that alcohol and benzodiazepines (sedative/hypnotics or central nervous system depressants) have comparable agonist-type effects upon receptors for GABA in the brain.

A similar approach for pharmacotherapeutic facilitation of abstinence substitutes the drug methadone for heroin. Both methadone and heroin activate endogenous opiate receptors, but methadone does so somewhat incompletely; methadone does not have the intense euphoric effect of heroin, but it can prevent the withdrawal symptoms that would normally follow abstinence from heroin. This methadone substitution pharmacotherapy has been somewhat successful for supporting abstinence and preventing relapse of heroin usage.

A heralded alternative pharmacological approach has not been so successful at sustaining abstinence. This less successful approach uses receptor antagonist drugs that completely block the euphoria induced by the abused drug, which acts as an agonist for those same receptors. One example is the attempted use of an opiate-receptor antagonist such as naltrexone to treat addiction to an opiate drug such as heroin. The idea here is that the pleasurable effect of heroin can be diminished or abolished by using a pharmacological treatment that blocks endogenous opiate receptors—the same receptors that mediate acute pleasurable consequences of heroin usage. This kind of approach had been touted as a potential "cure" for addiction, but it has generally failed to be effective in the clinical setting. The failure of this therapeutic approach is predictable if we take seriously the motivation for drug taking: pleasure. For example, if the typical drug user is highly motivated to use heroin to obtain the euphoria induced by it, why would he or she take a medication that blocks the ability of heroin to produce the euphoria that is so desired? The most likely outcome in this situation is that the addict in search of a heroin-induced euphoria will stop taking the medication that prevents that effect. Only when the motivation to take a medicinal drug that prevents the euphoria is greater than the motivation to take heroin (or some other drug) to get the euphoria will this pharmacological approach be useful to treat chronic substance usage. In short, the motivation to use a drug to experience its pleasurable effect is substantial and therefore quite resistant to treatment.

Considerable attention continues to focus on the use of pharmacotherapy approaches to sustain abstinence or prevent relapse of drug usage. Some of the recent attempts that focus on relapse prevention generally use a therapeutic drug that might diminish the appetite or craving for the pleasurable effects of the abused drug. There are several successful examples of this type of pharmacotherapy:

- The opiate receptor antagonist naltrexone (ReVia) has been used to delay relapse of use of alcohol.
- The drug buproprion (Wellbutrin), also successfully used to treat depression (presumably by altering serotonin and dopamine neurotransmission) can delay relapse of nicotine use in smokers attempting to quit.
- Buprenorphine (Buprenex, an incomplete or partial mu opiate receptor agonist drug) also has been used to inhibit craving for nicotine.

The successes of these drug treatments suggest that craving may have something to do with endogenous opiates, dopamine, and/or serotonin neurotransmission. Indeed, neuroimaging studies have detected blood flow/metabolic abnormalities in the orbitofrontal cortex that are correlated with craving (Table 11.1), and the orbitofrontal cortex is served by dopamine neurons (Figure 11.1). Just as a dysfunctional relation between the corpus striatum and the orbitofrontal cortex has been hypothesized to explain the intrusive thoughts of obsessive–compulsive disorder (OCD; Chapter 10), it is reasonable to propose that a dysfunctional striatum–orbitofrontal cortex (Table 11.1) process involving dopamine, serotonin, or endogenous opiates explains the intrusive thoughts related to drug craving. This possibility suggests a common neurochemical mechanism(s) for OCD and the chronic use of drugs.

> Jeff is an alcoholic—an addict for 6 years. He drank every single day. He has been sober for 4 years now, but he still thinks about drinking. The naltrexone therapy is the key for Jeff; so long as he takes his medication every day and continues to tolerate the nausea the naltrexone induces, he can resist the frequent urges to drink. But he needs his naltrexone. Jeff is not using alcohol, but he *is* drug-dependent.

The idea that relapse prevention can be achieved over the long term with chronic use of a pharmacotherapeutic substance merits one last comment. If addiction is a chronic, relapsing brain disease that is characterized by drug-induced permanent changes in brain neurochemistry, then the approach that uses a therapeutic drug daily, to successfully prevent relapse over the long term, is an approach that replaces one drug dependence (perhaps an illegal drug) with another drug dependence (the therapeutic drug). This pharmacological switching may have its advantages (e.g., in terms of legality, physiological risk, psychosocial issues), but it does not completely solve the problem of drug dependence for that addict.

Psychotherapy for Addiction

Psychotherapeutic techniques for disorders of substance use are necessary to support successful abstinence and to delay or prevent relapse. These approaches include virtually each and every category of talk therapy: from one-on-one therapist–client approaches to support group approaches. In essence, we know nothing about how these psychotherapeutic approaches alter the neurochemistry of the brain or peripheral physiological processes to achieve their positive outcomes specifically in the treatment of substance use disorders. It is worth noting, however, that cognitive–behavioral therapy has been demonstrated to decrease glucose metabolism (and presumably neuronal functioning) in the orbitofrontal cortex, caudate nucleus, and thalamus as symptoms of OCD are improved (Chapter 10). These findings may be relevant to psychotherapy for addiction if addicts and people with OCD share neurochemically similar dysfunction of the orbitofrontal cortex.

It would be a mistake, however, to expect that nonpharmacological talk therapy for addiction *must* target brain processes in order to be successful. The idea that problems of chronic substance use can be reduced to a neurochemical abnormality in the orbitofrontal cortex (or other sites) in the brain is a poor one, because a problem such as addiction appears in a person living in a unique environment, who is involved with his or her own social relationships and environmental–social stimuli that change as that former novice drug user becomes an addict. That addict is a product of interacting neurochemical, physiological, psychological, and social processes that may have contributed to the chronic drug usage. These complex processes may include genetically determined abnormal sensitivity to drugs, defective learning processes related to drug usage, frequency of social opportunities supporting drug usage, and frequency of exposure to environmental cues that elicit craving and compulsive behaviors. Some of these factors may be vulnerable to pharmacological treatment approaches that alter the brain or peripheral nervous system and physiology, but other factors may not. For example, pharmacological approaches may be developed that (1) alter sensitivity to drugs by targeting peripheral nervous system sensory processes or thalamus or hypothalamus; (2) alter learning about drug effects by targeting processes in hippocampus; or (3) diminish the impact of cues that elicit craving by targeting processes in the hippocampus or cortex. However, the contributing social factors may require nonpharmacological therapeutic interventions that offer advice that addresses an addict's ability to make decisions about where to live, where to visit, with whom to associate, and how to deal with environmental cues (people and places) that elicit craving and increase the likelihood of drug usage. In summary, combined drug and talk therapies may be necessary to address a problem such as addiction, and combined drug and talk therapies will be most effective when tailored to the specific needs of the individual.

Gender Differences in the Brain Related to Addiction/Dependence

The incidence of substance use disorders is generally greater in men than in women, with a ratio approximating 2:1 or 3:1; the ratio for alcohol use disorders is approximately 5:1 for men:women. In addition, women diagnosed with substance use disorders have a higher incidence than men of comorbid depressive and anxiety disorders. It is not likely that these gender differences in incidence are attributable exclusively to gender differences in the brain, but there are some interesting, potentially relevant differences in brain processes between men and women:

1. Women are more susceptible than men to the neurotoxic effect of MDMA on serotonin neurons.
2. The effects of chronic nicotine or cocaine use upon the upregulation of the serotonin presynaptic transport process is greater in women than men.
3. The effects of alcohol upon the downregulation of GABA receptors is greater in men.
4. Women have diminished capacity (compared to men) for metabolism of alcohol in the stomach.

These findings suggest that future efforts focused on gender differences in brain and physiology related to disorders of substance use are likely to reveal some interesting findings important for understanding the etiology of substance use disorders and for developing novel, gender-specific therapeutic approaches.

Perspective

The use of drugs that have addictive potential has acute and long-term effects upon the neurochemistry of dopamine (and other neurochemicals) in the brain, resulting in a reorganization of neuronal processes in brain that (1) supports orbitofrontal cortex-mediated, compulsive drug-seeking and usage characteristic of addiction/dependence; and (2) may increase the vulnerability to other psychiatric disorders such as depression, anxiety, or psychosis—disorders involving abnormalities in neuro-transmitter systems (dopamine, serotonin, norepinephrine, GABA,) that can be altered by many addictive drugs. In addition, the fact that addictive drugs provide rapid, potent activation of many of the same neuronal processes in brain that are involved in all behaviors that bring pleasure suggests that resistance to treatment for substance use disorders is highly likely. Research efforts in animals and humans that measure the acute and long-term neurochemical effects of recreational psychoactive drugs should reveal new neurochemical and neuroanatomical targets for combined pharmacotherapeutic and psychotherapeutic strategies for treatment of dysfunctional behaviors in substance users. These combined therapeutic strategies will likely be most effective when altering processes in the brain as well as improving the ability of the recovering addict to make good decisions about how to respond to social and environmental factors that encourage drug usage.

12

Overeating

Overeating is only one of several factors that contributes to becoming overweight or obese. Eating, together with inherited tendencies to store more or less body fat, social and cultural factors that support choices about when, what, and how much to eat (or drink), and patterns of physical exertion all contribute to the likelihood of gaining weight. The formula for weight gain is simple: Greater ingestion than expenditure of calories is likely to result in weight gain. Within that framework, let's focus on this question: What processes in the brain directly contribute to eating behavior in humans?

> Carole had already eaten enough calories during lunch at Tino's to cover at least 100% of her daily needs, but the idea of eating an éclair dripping with melted chocolate sauce and a generous dollop of homemade creamy vanilla ice cream simply could not be resisted. She could already taste it just thinking about it. She didn't need it, but she wanted it. The chocolate and ice cream would feel so very good in her mouth!

As reasonable as it seems that the brain would organize eating behavior in a manner that would ensure sufficient intake of calories and prevent excessive intake, thereby maintaining some optimum body weight, the fact that the brain also has neurochemical processes that serve pleasure invalidates that supposition. In fact, it appears that behaviors of fundamental importance for survival (e.g., sexual behavior, eating, drinking fluids) are behaviors that facilitate release of dopamine into synapses of the nucleus accumbens, a process identified (Chapter 11) as one of the brain-mediated mechanisms for the psychological experience of pleasure.

To think about how the brain and nervous system organize the pleasurable activity of eating, consider a system in which three sets of brain processes are important for coordinating eating behavior: (1) processes that initiate eating when a need for calories (fuels) is detected; (2) processes that slow and stop eating when an abundance of ingested calories is detected; and (3) processes to signal delight when tasty substances are placed into the mouth for ingestion. Finally, the functioning of each of these sets of processes is adjusted by mechanisms that monitor stores of body fat.

Brain Processes for Hunger and the Initiation of Eating

Although the brain does not have a single group of localized neurons that could be described as a "hunger center" (see Chapter 1), a number of neurochemicals are located in numerous sites in the brain (and the autonomic nervous system serving the gastrointestinal tract; see Figures 5.1 and 5.4) that appear to serve the role of initiating eating behavior. Among these are neurochemicals that have an extraordinary potency for stimulating food intake in animals; for example, neuropeptide Y (NPY). The fact that NPY in the arcuate nucleus and paraventricular nucleus (PVN) of the hypothalamus can powerfully stimulate eating (of carbohydrate-rich foods, in particular) does not make NPY the "hunger signal," just as it does not make the arcuate/paraventricular hypothalamic area the "hunger center." It does identify NPY as one among numerous neurochemical factors that contribute to the initiation of eating (Table 12.1). Being able to identify such neurochemicals and their sites of action in the brain provides neurochemical and neuroanatomical targets for potential therapeutic interventions for increasing or decreasing food intake.

Among the various neurochemicals and brain sites that appear to be involved in the initiation of eating and the control of meal size, it is possible to identify (in some cases) the calorie- or fuel-related deficit that provokes the process. For example, when blood glucose declines following a period of food deprivation, activity of NPY neurons (in arcuate/PVN) is increased, leading to the initiation of eating. This endogenous NPY neurochemical signal for eating can be modulated (i.e., enhanced or diminished by blood-borne leptin or insulin) in proportion to the degree of body fat deficit (or surplus). For example, in someone who had recently gained body weight due to an increase in stored body fat, the greater fat

Table 12.1
**Endogenous Neurochemicals Important for Hunger and Satiety and
Their Presumed Sites of Action in the Brain**

Endogenous Neurochemical	Site of Action
Hunger	
Anandamide	Nucleus accumbens, hippocampus
Beta-endorphin	Arcuate nucleus
Dynorphin	Arcuate nucleus, PVN
GABA	Nucleus accumbens, VTA
Galanin	PVN
Ghrelin	Arcuate nucleus, PVN
Growth hormone releasing hormone	Suprachiasmatic nucleus
Neuropeptide Y	Arcuate nucleus, PVN
Orexin	Lateral hypothalamus
Norepinephrine	Nucleus acccumbens, hypothalamus
Peptide YY	PVN, hippocampus
Satiety	
Acetylcholine	Nucleus accumbens
Amylin	Hypothalamus
Bombesin	Amygdala
Cholecystokinin	PVN
Corticotropin releasing hormone	PVN
Dopamine	Nucleus accumbens
Enterostatin	Amygdala, PVN
Glucagon	PVN
Alpha-melanocyte-stimulating hormone	Arcuate nucleus
Neurotensin	PVN
Serotonin	Arcuate nucleus, PVN
Somatostatin	Suprachiasmatic nucleus
Body-Fat-Sensitive Modulators of Hunger and Satiety	
Leptin	Arcuate nucleus
Insulin	Arcuate nucleus, PVN

Note. Presumed sites of action are determined from research in animals. Many of these endogenous neurochemicals also have effects upon peripheral physiology that are likely to affect eating behavior. Abbreviations: PVN, paraventricular nucleus of the hypothalamus; VTA, ventral tegmental area; GABA, gamma-aminobutyric acid.

content would increase leptin in the blood. This increased leptin would, in turn, decrease the ability of NPY to stimulate eating when food deprivation provokes the release of NPY into synapses within the arcuate nucleus in the brain. This type of interaction between NPY and leptin is an example of a mechanism by which body fat content can provide a blood-borne signal (leptin or insulin) to the brain to modulate the potency of a neurochemical hunger signal (NPY) to affect the size of a meal.

The ability of the brain to detect deficits in glucose or decreases in body fat requires obtaining information from the body, either through the blood (e.g., leptin, insulin) or from those elements of the autonomic nervous system that organize functions of peripheral organs (Figures 5.1 and 5.4), and therefore must be able to transmit sensory information from those peripheral organs to the brainstem and then to the hypothalamus. Just as the brain and peripheral gastrointestinal processes work together to coordinate initiation of eating and food intake, so too do brain and peripheral processes coordinate the slowing and cessation of eating that occur as the eater becomes satisfied.

Brain Processes for Satiety

The placing of food into the mouth, followed by chewing, swallowing, and the passage of food into the stomach and then into the small intestine are events that are detected by various sensory cells in the oropharynx, gastrointestinal tract, and other abdominal organs that inform the brain (Figure 5.4) that food is being ingested and calories are being processed. These numerous signals of peripheral origin (including taste, stomach fullness, cholecystokinin; Chapter 5), acting through sensory neurons in the sympathetic and parasympathetic components of the autonomic nervous system (Figure 5.1), activate neuronal processes in the brainstem, thalamus, and hypothalamus that integrate the activity of a variety of satiety signals for slowing and stopping eating behavior. As you can guess by now, these signals do not comprise a single neurochemical "satiety signal" activated in a single "satiety center" in the brain. Instead, satiety (much like hunger) can be viewed as a psychological process that is the result of the integration of multiple neurochemical signals (Table 12.1) activated in proportion to the ongoing ingestion of various constituents that provide fuels for the brain and body. Furthermore, as we saw for the hunger signal NPY, the potency of some satiety signals (e.g., cholecystokinin; CCK) can be adjusted by blood-borne leptin in proportion to the storage of fuel as body fat. For example, in someone who has recently gained body weight due to an increase in stored body fat, the greater fat content would increase leptin in blood. This increased leptin would, in turn, increase the ability of CCK to slow and stop eating when CCK is released as ingested food reaches the intestine.

Although it has been a popular notion for decades that stopping eating in response to feelings of satiety is a process activated by the brain to prevent an excess intake of fuels (which would be stored as fat), and that eating when hungry is a process activated by the brain to repair a deficit in fuels, it appears that the pleasure of eating or the incentive value of foods also plays an important role in the ability of the brain to coordinate feeding behavior.

Brain Processes That Mediate Incentive Value of Foods

Not much has gone well for Kate during the past several months. Her best friend moved to Chicago, Kate's work for the law firm has been less than fulfilling, there's not much worth seeing at the cinema, and she's feeling a bit lonely sitting home at night. The one source of pleasure and delight that she can count on, however, is usually right there in the cupboard. Whether it's a bag of potato chips and dip, or a plate of homemade cookies, when those things are chewed and swallowed, it does feel good. Kate doesn't need to be hungry to enjoy eating those items. She feels that she eats them to be momentarily excited by the tastes.

The tastiness or palatability of food is important for brain processes that coordinate eating behavior. Foods that are fatty or sweet (regardless of nutritional or caloric value) activate neurochemical processes in the brain that are related to pleasure. The more potent a food is for activating a release of dopamine or endogenous opioids in the synapses of the nucleus accumbens, the more likely it is that an animal or a human will ingest that food for its ability to bring pleasure. It is quite evident that people do avidly consume pleasant-tasting substances having great caloric value or having little or no caloric value; examples of the latter include low-calorie, diet soft drinks and foods sweetened with artificial, noncaloric sweeteners. It appears then, that nutritional value, caloric deficits, and caloric surpluses aside, eating behavior may represent, in many circumstances, eating to experience tasty foods that bring pleasure. We all know that a mere look at the pastry on the counter is enough to tell you that it will feel good when placed into your mouth. And you know that if it feels good in the mouth, the tendency is to take another bite!

In summary, the brain coordinates eating behavior through an integration of processes that normally protect us from loss or gain of body fat due to caloric deficit or surfeit, with processes that mediate pleasure. The presence of a caloric deficit may be sufficient to elicit eating behavior of a food that has high incentive value (cheesecake) or low incentive value (plain toasted bread). The absence of a caloric deficit may not prevent eating behavior when a person is presented with a food that has high incentive value, but the absence of a caloric deficit may preclude eating a relatively unpalatable food. Moreover, the presence of a caloric surplus, which normally slows or stops eating, may not prevent eating if the person is presented with a food that has a high incentive value. Thus, physiological factors correlated with caloric deficits, surfeits, and body fat content interact with incentive value of available foods to determine what and how much is eaten.

So what exactly accounts for overeating? Within the framework presented above, overeating can by hypothesized to result from one, or some interacting combination, of the following factors:

1. Increased activity of one or more neurochemical signals for hunger that results in increased frequency of eating or ingestion of bigger meals.
2. Diminished activity of one or more neurochemical signals for satiety that results in failure to stop eating, resulting in bigger meals or increased frequency of eating.
3. Diminished capacity of a modulator (assessing body fat content) to inhibit the effect of a hunger signal or to enhance the effect of a satiety signal.
4. Excessive use of food to increase activation of brain neurochemical pleasure processes.

Overeating as a Substance Use Disorder

Ingestion of palatable foods and ingestion of addictive drugs share the ability to provoke the release of dopamine (and in some cases, endogenous opioids) from neurons in the nucleus accumbens. Is this merely a coincidence, or does eating palatable foods and using addictive drugs represent two different ways of activating the same neurochemical process(es)? Is it reasonable to consider overeating to be a type of substance use disorder?

There is behavioral evidence to support this idea. The following characteristics are shared by eating and addiction disorders:

- Eating or use of a drug can be comforting, thereby relieving stress.
- Preoccupation (obsessing) about food or drugs may include craving.
- Overeating or drug taking can persist despite negative consequences.
- Guilt often follows the excessive use of food or a drug.
- Overeaters and addicts deny having "a problem."
- Maintaining diminished intake (abstinence) is very difficult; i.e., relapse rates are high.

Other factors that link overeating and addiction include the high comorbidity of eating disorders and substance use disorders and evident heritability of vulnerability for addicts and for the obese.

Still further similarities between overeating and drug usage are found in neuroimaging studies comparing the brains of addicts with those of the obese: Chronic users of cocaine, methamphetamine, or heroin and obese humans have downregulation of dopamine D2 receptors in the brain. In addicts this downregulation has been linked to a dysfunctional orbitofrontal cortex, which leads to craving. In the obese downregulated D2 receptors may represent diminished sensitivity to rewarding stimuli such as palatable food. This diminished sensitivity may require that larger meals, or more frequent meals, or meals rich in fats and sweets need to be eaten in order to feel satisfied. This idea is consistent with the finding in obese humans of abnormally increased glucose metabolism near the postcentral gyrus of the parietal cortex—that area of sensory cortex receiving information regarding palatability from the mouth, lips, and tongue.

These assorted findings suggest that food can be used as effectively as an addictive drug for activating brain processes associated with pleasure (Figure 11.1), and for reorganizing the brain in a manner that leads to compulsive ingestion. If this is true, it is not so surprising to see that eating and substance use disorders often coexist. It is also reasonable to think that overeating or drug taking are ways to self-medicate a dopamine neurotransmission system that has diminished sensitivity, and that these kinds of self-medicating ingestive behaviors then create the brain of a substance (food or drug) use disorder.

Disturbances in the brain processes (and peripheral nervous system) that control hunger, satiety, and the pleasure-producing palatability of food may interact to contribute to overeating. Information from studies (in animals and humans) of these brain and peripheral physiological processes in the control of eating has provided useful ideas for therapeutic interventions (including pharmacotherapy, psychotherapy, and surgical manipulation of peripheral organs such as the stomach) to reduce appetite and produce loss of weight. What might effective pharmacotherapeutic approaches further reveal about brain processes related to overeating?

Pharmacotherapy for Treating Overeating

Drugs that alter neurotransmission of dopamine, norepinephrine, and serotonin have been successfully used to reduce appetite and produce loss of weight. One of the first drugs to be used in this way was amphetamine, which can enhance release from presynaptic nerve terminals and inhibit presynaptic reuptake processes of each of these neurotransmitters. How this potent mix of neurochemical consequences of amphetamine inhibits appetite is not entirely clear, because dopamine, norepinephrine, and serotonin neurons have widespread distribution throughout the brain (see Figures 9.1, 9.2, and 11.1), providing amphetamine with multiple sites for its potential actions, including (but not limited to) the nucleus accumbens and hypothalamus (Table 12.1). Despite the potency of amphetamine for inhibiting appetite, tolerance develops, requiring repeated increases in dosage across weeks and months, until dosages large enough to induce psychosis are being used. This alarming fact led the FDA to prohibit the prescribed use of amphetamine for reduction of appetite.

The pharmacological heir apparent to amphetamine for potent inhibition of appetite was the combination of drugs known as fen/phen— fenfluramine and phentermine. This combination provides a less complicated mix of effects upon dopamine and serotonin neurotransmission that is effective for reducing appetite and producing loss of weight. However, the discovery of potentially lethal side effects of fen/phen upon cardiovascular processes quickly led to the demise of this combination as pharmacotherapy for overeating and obesity.

Touted as an answer to the fen/phen clinical failure is sibutramine (Meridia), a potent inhibitor of presynaptic reuptake of serotonin and, to a lesser extent, dopamine. One potential problem for the clinical use of sibutramine is the simple fact that the percentage of weight loss may not be sufficiently impressive (between 5 and 10%) to outweigh the risks of the associated side effects.

Each of these pharmacotherapeutic approaches is consistent with the research in animals and humans that has demonstrated the involvement of dopamine, serotonin and norepinephrine processes in eating behavior (Table 12.1). Given the widespread distribution of these brain processes (see Figures 9.1, 9.2, and 11.1), it is not surprising that these pharmacotherapeutic approaches, which affect large and diverse areas of the brain and peripheral nervous system, might ultimately be doomed by problems of unwanted drug-induced side effects.

Greater success for pharmacotherapy to reduce appetite may be found in pharmacologically more selective modulation of neurotransmission. For example, the endogenous neurochemicals identified as important for hunger (Table 12.1) and the initiation of eating (e.g., peptide YY, NPY, galanin, dynorphin, beta-endorphin, growth hormone releasing hormone, anandamide, GABA, ghrelin) may provide opportunities for development of therapeutic drugs that act as selective antagonists for their receptor subtypes (e.g., the drug rimonabant [Accomplia], a CB1 cannabinoid receptor antagonist). Likewise, the endogenous neurochemicals identified as involved in satiety for food and cessation of eating (e.g., alpha-melanocyte-stimulating hormone, neurotensin, corticotropin releasing hormone, cholecystokinin, glucagon, enterostatin, amylin, bombesin, somatostatin) and the blood-borne chemicals (leptin, insulin) that modulate satiety (and hunger) signals in proportion to body fat content may provide opportunities for the development of therapeutic drugs that act as selective agonists for their respective receptor subtypes.

As logical as the above suggestions seem, however, there is a problem regarding the ultimate clinical effectiveness of a drug that can selectively alter one of numerous neurochemical signals for hunger or satiety: If hunger (or satiety) is normally a product of the interaction of a dozen or so endogenous neurochemical signals, how can the selective manipulation of only one have a meaningful impact upon hunger (or satiety)? It is likely that a selective manipulation of one small part of the system (having built-in redundancy) will be compensated for by a change in the contribution made by the other (nonmanipulated) parts of the system, perhaps resulting in no net effect upon eating behavior. And, yes, this argument can be extended to make the case that there cannot be a single drug that will effectively and safely reduce appetite when used over an extended period of time.

Psychotherapy for Treating Overeating

Nondrug treatments for weight loss and maintenance of weight loss are considered essential, especially in view of the fact that there is no effective and safe drug therapy for overeating. These treatments, which range from psychotherapy to dieting regimens to support groups, generally are successful when they manage to help a client make significant changes in lifestyle or in his or her "relationship" with food. Such changes might include strategies for avoiding risky eating environments (e.g., The Dinosaur Bar-B-Q in Syracuse, New York) and environmental cues that elicit poor decisions, craving, and overeating.

Essentially nothing is known about how these nondrug therapeutic approaches affect the brain when they are successfully used to reduce eating. The exception may be found in what is known about a few psychotherapeutic approaches (e.g., cognitive–behavioral therapy) that have been used to treat disorders of mood, anxiety, and substance use (Chapters 9, 10, and 11), and which also have demonstrated effects upon brain processes when treating substance use (see Chapter 11). If these psychotherapy-induced effects upon the brain also occur when the same psychotherapy is used to treat overeating, then we could speculate that psychotherapy may be affecting brain processes when diminished overeating is the outcome.

Gender Differences Related to Overeating

There are gender-related differences for a variety of neurochemicals, including dopamine, serotonin, and endogenous opioids. It is not clear how these gender differences might account for differences between men and women regarding overeating. But the fact that there are rather astounding differences between genders in the incidence of disorders such as anorexia and bulimia implicates the gender-related differences in the brain or peripheral physiology. This is an area of research ripe for discovery of interesting findings.

Perspective

Eating too much can contribute to varying degrees of overweight and obesity. Eating too much may be the consequence of one or several abnormalities in the processes of the brain and nervous system that coordinate hunger and satiety. These processes utilize numerous endogenous neurochemicals in several areas of the brain (in particular, arcuate nucleus, PVN, and nucleus accumbens) that mediate hunger, satiety, and pleasure related to eating. Easy access to a variety of foods may lead to the ingestion of palatable foods that activate brain processes involved in pleasure; in turn, these pleasure-related processes might dominate the processes that control eating to repair fuel deficits or to prevent surfeits, perhaps leading to the compulsive ingestion of food that contributes to overweight and obesity. Future options for the treatment of overeating should include novel pharmacotherapeutic approaches that alter one or several mechanisms of hunger, satiety, and pleasure, and psychotherapeutic approaches that encourage the making of wise decisions regarding exactly what and how much is placed into one's mouth and permitted within the cupboards of one's kitchen.

13

Bulimia and Anorexia

Disturbances in eating behavior are the most prominent features of anorexia nervosa and bulimia nervosa, each of which is classified as an "eating disorder" in the DSM. But eating too little or eating too much is not an adequate description of anorexia or bulimia, respectively. Both anorexia and bulimia are chronic, disabling disorders marked by abnormalities in eating and distorted attitudes and perceptions regarding body shape and weight, among other psychological, social, and physiological disturbances. These two disorders occur much more frequently in women than in men; these differences in vulnerability may be partially attributable to gender-based differences in the brain.

> Trish bore the guilt pretty well after again telling a lie to get away from the table so that she could vomit without anyone knowing. Why bother discussing it with them? They wouldn't understand it from her perspective. They just wouldn't believe some of what she wanted to confide in them— the feeling that she was fat and ugly; the junk food she had hidden in shoeboxes in her closet; the use of laxatives; the fear, real fear, of being unable to stop eating once she had begun. And they certainly would think she was crazy when trying to convince them that she had no real control over her eating.

Bulimia

The relatively rapid eating of large quantities of highly caloric foods (i.e., binge eating) followed by purging through self-induced vomiting (or the use of a laxative) are two hallmark characteristics of bulimia nervosa.

These bingeing and purging behaviors are often accompanied by low self-esteem, depression or anxiety, denial or secretiveness, reports of no satisfaction after eating, negative body image, fear of not being able to stop eating, and drug usage. This list suggests a clinical picture that is considerably more complicated than simply an "eating disorder" in which too much food is being eaten. In fact, some of the non-food-related features of the disorder are indicative of personality disturbances, anxiety, obsessions, compulsions, depression, and substance abuse, each of which can coexist with bulimia nervosa. Is it helpful or is it misleading to view bulimia as a disorder of specifically eating behavior, or as a disorder in which all non-food-related symptoms are secondary to those of dysfunctional eating, hunger, or satiety?

One way to address this question is to consider whether the wealth of information regarding the physiological and neurochemical control of eating is helpful for understanding and treating all symptoms of bulimia, particularly those involving the inappropriate use of food. Questions such as the following may lead the way:

Which of the many interacting control mechanisms of eating (or satiety) are malfunctioning in the bulimic?
Which of the neurochemical processes in the brain are malfunctioning in a manner that would lead to eating in binges?
Does binge eating represent the diminished effectiveness of one (or several) neurochemical signals for satiety?
Does binge eating represent the hyperactivity of one (or several) neurochemical signals for hunger?
Is binge eating a self-medicating behavior that activates a neurochemical signal for pleasure to correct a deficiency in a dopamine or endogenous opioid pleasure process?
Do we know enough about the brain and bulimia to adequately answer any of these questions?

Attempts to identify specific neurochemical abnormalities in the brain and physiology of bulimics have led to relatively little understanding. One of the more interesting findings is the abnormally low level of cholecystokinin (CCK) in their blood following a meal: Deficient release of CCK during a meal (one among numerous signals for satiety; Table 12.1), correlates with bulimics' reports of abdominal discomfort and diminished satiety and lack of pleasure in eating a meal. These reports are consistent with findings of a slower emptying of ingested food from the stomach into the intestine, leading to an exaggerated sense of fullness in the stomach and the delayed release of CCK due to food reaching the small intestine at a slower than normal rate. Moreover, the ability of released CCK to induce satiety depends, in part, upon sensory neurons in the abdominal vagus nerve (Figure 5.4), which shows abnormal activity in bulimics. Finally, the deficient post-meal blood levels of CCK and the diminished post-meal satiety in bulimics appear to be related, because they both can be improved by pharmacotherapy using an antidepressant drug (e.g., the tricyclic antidepressant desipramine).

Although deficient release of a satiety signal such as CCK may explain some aspects of the binge eating and abnormal feelings of satiety, it is not likely that disturbances in the gastric emptying of food, deficient release of CCK, and abnormal activation of sensory neurons in the peripheral parasympathetic autonomic nervous system (Figure 5.1) can explain the entire constellation of psychological abnormalities that can accompany binge eating and purging in bulimics. In addition, it is not clear what (if anything) is abnormal in the brain regarding the effect of CCK upon satiety. In fact, little is known about abnormalities in the brain during bulimia, other than neuroimaging reports (Table 13.1) of abnormalities in glucose metabolism in the amygdala and frontal, temporal, cingulate, and parietal cortices—areas of the brain served by several neurotransmitters, including norepinephrine, serotonin, and dopamine.

The fact that antidepressant drug-induced alteration of neurotransmitters can diminish symptoms of bulimia may reveal associated disordered brain processes. For example, the demonstration that the antidepressant-induced improvement in symptoms of bulimia is not secondary to the relief of depressive symptoms, reveals that symptoms of bulimia may be related to disturbances in specific neurochemical processes that are, to some degree, distinct from the neurochemical disturbances underlying depression, and that the neurochemical disturbances of depression are not necessarily the cause of bulimia. To further illustrate this point, we could speculate that serotonin neurons serving the hypothalamus and cortex may be the culprits in the brain of a bulimic, whereas serotonin neurons serving the cortex, amygdala, and hippocampus may be the culprits in the brain of a depressive (Figure 9.2).

Support for the idea of the involvement of serotonin in both bulimia and depression includes the finding of downregulation of serotonin 5HT-2A receptors in the medial orbitofrontal cortex of recovered bulimics (Table 13.1), and the downregulation of 5HT-2A receptors in people successfully treated with pharmacotherapy for depression (Table 5.1). Also consistent with the idea of underlying neurochemical abnormalities in bulimia and depression is the fact that antidepressant drugs in multiple classes (tricyclics, SSRIs, MAOIs) can be effective in treating symptoms of bulimia. The ability of SSRIs to improve symptoms of bulimia is also interesting, given that serotonin has a role in satiety, probably through activation of the vagus nerve and through the activity of serotonin in the hypothalamus (Table 12.1).

Table 13.1
Reported Abnormalities in Brains of Humans with Bulimia or Anorexia

Bulimia	Anorexia
Fewer 5HT-2A receptors in orbitofrontal cortex (bulimia in remission)	More 5HT-1A serotonin receptors in: Raphe nucleus Cortex Temporal cortex (amygdala, hippocampus) Striatum
More 5HIAA serotonin metabolite in CSF	
Decrease in blood flow/metabolism in: Amygdala Frontal cortex Temporal cortex Cingulate cortex Parietal cortex	Fewer 5HT-2A serotonin receptors in: Temporal cortex (amygdala, hippocampus) Cingulate cortex Sensory–motor cortex Occipital–parietal cortex
	More 5HIAA serotonin metabolite in CSF
	Less HVA dopamine metabolite in CSF
	More neuropeptide Y in CSF
	Abnormalities in blood flow/metabolism in: Frontal cortex Cingulate cortex Parietal cortex

Note. Reported abnormalities are apparent in recovered anorexics and bulimics; i.e., the abnormalities are not secondary to change in body weight. Abbreviations: 5HIAA, 5-hydroxyindoleacetic acid; 5HT, 5-hydroxytryptamine (serotonin); HVA, homovanillic acid; CSF, cerebrospinal fluid.

In addition to the evidence that two neurochemical signals for satiety (CCK, serotonin) may contribute to some aspects of bulimia, there is also evidence that leptin, a neurochemical that can modulate various satiety and hunger signals (Table 12.1), is deficient in the blood of bulimics. Moreover, the blood levels of leptin appear to be inversely correlated with the frequency of binge eating episodes.

A deficiency in the ability of leptin to modulate a dopamine-mediated signal to the brain that is activated by the incentive value of highly palatable foods may also contribute to bulimia: If deficiency of leptin establishes a diminished ability of ingested food to activate a dopamine- (or opioid-) mediated pleasure process in the brain, then a binge may represent a behavior that may "correct" that neurochemical deficiency. The idea here is that an abnormally larger quantity of palatable food must be eaten to achieve a normal level of a dopamine/pleasure process in the brain of a bulimic than in the brain of a nonbulimic. This explanation characterizes an eating binge as the excessive use of a substance (food) to activate a dopamine (or opioid)/pleasure process in the brain, suggesting that some of the behavioral and neurochemical aspects of bulimia may resemble processes that are dysfunctional in chronic drug users or abusers.

In summary, neurochemicals in the body (CCK, leptin) and in the brain (serotonin, dopamine) appear to be involved in some portion of the symptoms of bulimia nervosa. It is not at all clear, however, that abnormalities in these neurochemical signals that are related to eating behavior and feelings of satiety represent the principal abnormalities that underlie this complex disorder, with its multiple physiological, psychological, and social dimensions. Given this lack of certainty regarding physiological mechanisms, it is not so surprising that, despite the effectiveness of some antidepressant drugs in treating bulimia (in particular, for bulimics with comorbid anxiety or depression), it is generally the case that pharmacotherapy is *less* effective than psychotherapy (or combined psychotherapy and pharmacotherapy) for treating bulimia (and binge-eating disorder; i.e., bingeing without purging).

Of the various psychotherapeutic approaches that have been assessed in clinical trials, cognitive–behavioral therapy has been demonstrated to be the most consistently successful treatment of bulimia. The fact that cognitive–behavioral therapy combined with pharmacotherapy sometimes can produce greater benefit than could be gained using either therapeutic approach alone, suggests that these two treatment approaches may improve bulimia through different physiological or neurochemical processes (see discussion on this issue in Chapter 9). The identity of these neurochemical processes remains to be determined, although we do know that cognitive–behavioral therapy for the treatment of OCD (Chapter 10) appears to alter serotonin neurotransmission in the orbitofrontal cortex, caudate, and thalamus.

Anorexia

Perhaps even more so than in the case of bulimia nervosa, abnormalities related to personality, perceptions, and mood are also evident in anorexia nervosa. The anorexic's obsession about not gaining weight, the compulsive restriction of eating behavior, the frequently accompanying perfectionism, depression, anxiety, and denial—all suggest that anorexia is far from being simply a disorder involving eating.

> Nancy was hungry "all of the time," and she enjoyed planning meals and preparing food for others. However, she was sensationally capable of restricting her own eating. "No one is better than I am at controlling my eating," she would boastfully confide to friends. She had perfected the art of imposing restrictions upon her eating behavior as one of the numerous perfections she had attained in her life—the regimented, arrangement of cans and jars on the cupboard shelves, the impeccable hair style, the exquisitely-manicured garden.

Hindered by the numerous physiological abnormalities that are measurable consequences of starvation and extreme loss of body weight, the search for underlying physiological or neurochemical causes of anorexia has provided little understanding that is useful for developing new therapeutic approaches. Antidepressant drugs (tricyclics, SSRIs) can be helpful in treating anorexia, and the SSRI fluoxetine (Prozac) has been used successfully to prevent relapse of anorexia, but there is no convincing evidence that anorexia is a behavioral disorder reflecting underlying disturbances *principally* in serotonin or norepinpehrine neurochemistry. There are, however, reports of abnormalities in the brain of anorexics that involve monoamine neurochemistry (Table 13.1): For example, in recovered food-restricting anorexics there is a downregulation of serotonin

5HT-2A receptors in the temporal cortex (and underlying amygdala and hippocampus) and the cingulate, sensorimotor, and occipital/parietal cortices. Moreover, there is an upregulation of serotonin 5HT-1A receptors in the raphe nucleus (an area rich in norepinephrine neurons) and in cortical, limbic, and striatal areas.

In addition to these measured abnormalities in the brain, there are reports of abnormalities in leptin levels in the blood, consistent with the reduced body fat seen in anorexics. And there is evidence of aversion to foods high in fat content, suggesting that fatty foods are less pleasant to eat for anorexics and perhaps less able to affect dopamine processes in the brain (Table 13.1) related to pleasure (Figure 11.1).

An alternative to this hypothesis that eating is less able to activate dopamine/pleasure processes in the brain of an anorexic is the idea that anorexics use other behavioral means to activate such processes. For example, excessive and ritualistic exercise, which is correlated with increased dopamine neurotransmission, may serve as a "substitute" for eating-elicited activation of dopamine neurotransmission. This exercise-induced activation of dopamine processes in the brain may be further enhanced by the starvation that results from restriction of eating.

The failure of anorexics to eat sufficient quantities of food to maintain normal body weight appears not to be due to a deficiency in neurochemical signals for hunger, because anorexics report being hungry *while* they are restricting their eating behavior. The compulsiveness regarding restriction of eating and exercising routines, together with the obsessive worry about remaining thin and the tendencies of perfectionism, suggest that anorexia nervosa may be more usefully regarded as an obsessive–compulsive type of anxiety disorder than an eating disorder resulting from decreased hunger or increased satiety. Unlike people treated for OCD, however, and despite documented abnormalities in monoamine processes in the brain, anorexics (as well as bulimics) tend to respond more favorably to psychotherapy than to pharmacotherapy. Therapeutic approaches that focus upon the abnormalities of personality and obsessions/compulsions tend to be more useful in the long term than are those therapies that focus specifically upon abnormal eating behavior.

The continuing search for the factors in the brain and nervous system that are related to the complexity of symptoms of anorexia nervosa may benefit from consideration of the typically adolescent age of onset and the fact that most diagnosed anorexics are young women and not men:

There certainly are differences between genders in the physiological, psychological, and social developmental processes occurring during adolescence, including the hypothalamus–pituitary axis, which regulates maturation of reproductive organs. This area of brain (and associated peripheral physiological processes) may hold the keys to understanding the neurochemical dysfunctions of anorexia nervosa for several reasons. First, the hypothalamus is certainly involved in eating behavior (Table 12.1). Second, the hypothalamus is served by monoamine neurotransmitters such as serotonin and norepinephrine (Figures 9.1 and 9.2). Third, serotonin and norepinephrine also have roles related to symptoms of anxiety (Chapter 10) that are so often seen in the anorexic. Reaching a better understanding of differences between genders in the maturation of neurochemical processes serving the hypothalamus–pituitary axis, considered within the broader context of psychological and social stressors appearing during adolescence, may reveal much about the mysteries of brain processes in anorexia nervosa.

Finally, more work must be done to investigate the way in which cultural issues or societal norms and expectations regarding body shape and weight have an impact upon neurochemical processes in the brain that then lead to the development of anorexia (or bulimia). Although it is reasonable to hypothesize that excessive contemplation and worry about physical appearance is a greater burden for young women than for most men, and that such burdensome thoughts can alter brain neurochemistry in a way that leads to psychopathology, evidence to demonstrate that this indeed is the case requires further study of the brain and behavior in humans.

Perspective

Bulimia and anorexia are disorders involving disturbances in mood, perception, and cognition that also feature dysfunctional eating behaviors as symptoms. The abnormalities in eating (and their consequences upon body weight) are so prominent that they have encouraged the conceptualizing of bulimia and anorexia as "eating disorders" likely to have abnormalities in the brain processes underlying hunger and satiety that control eating behavior. However, more than 50 years of productive research in animals and humans exploring the physiological and neurochemical processes involved in eating behavior have revealed relatively little that is helpful for understanding the physiological and neurochemical processes that contribute to the development of anorexia or bulimia. One explanation for this apparent disconnection is the idea that the study of physiological control mechanisms of eating may be somewhat irrelevant to understanding the full complexity of the behavioral, psychological, and social abnormalities of anorexia or bulimia, because these disorders have been incorrectly perceived as eating disorders. They most assuredly are disorders in which dysfunctional eating behavior is a prominent feature; there are abnormalities in some of the neurochemical processes related to eating, and some of the effective pharmacological treatments do alter neurochemical processes that control eating. Nevertheless, it may be more productive to conceive of (or to reclassify) these disorders as something other than eating disorders in order to redirect the search for their underlying brain processes. For example, greater emphasis upon features of these disorders such as disturbances in mood (anxiety, depression, obsessions/compulsions), personality, or substance use and abuse may prove to be more productive in guiding research strategies (including neuroimaging techniques) toward the assessment of neurochemical processes known to be involved in those non-food-related disorders (including serotonin, dopamine, GABA). What is now known and what is yet to be discovered about brain processes in depression, anxiety, and substance use disorders, including how these processes have an impact upon eating behavior, may be of central importance for understanding dysfunctional brain processes in anorexia and bulimia.

14

Attention-Deficit/Hyperactivity Disorder

ADHD has long been recognized as a chronic, disabling behavioral disorder warranting diagnosis and treatment. Boys generally are more active than girls, but when hyperactivity is extreme, it can cause difficulty in paying attention, which is a prerequisite for effective learning. A persistent pattern of extreme hyperactivity, inattention, impulsivity, and difficulty learning is diagnosed as attention-deficit/hyperactivity disorder (ADHD) between three and six times more frequently in boys than in girls. This diagnosis is properly made when the disorderly pattern of behavior seriously impairs the ability of a child (or adult) to function successfully in school, social relations, or at home. Making an appropriate diagnosis can be difficult when there is confusion regarding the "mean-

For a moment he imagined he was inside of a pinball machine dodging the steel ball as it bounced along the rubber bumpers and flippers. But the ball was Teddy and the bumpers were toys, and the flippers were other children in the living room. Six children between the ages of 4 and 7 were playing with one another and using the various toys in the living room. But Teddy stood out. Teddy began with one toy and as soon as he was distracted by the sound of a child playing with another, he dropped what he was doing and ran across the room to engage in a new task. This happened so frequently that it appeared to this observer that Teddy was living his life at twice the speed of normal. And it gradually became clear that the other children were not enjoying Teddy's lack of focus; they couldn't seem to get Teddy to stay with them, and they couldn't predict what Teddy would do next. In fact, it didn't appear that Teddy could predict what Teddy would do next.

ing" of specific dysfunctional behaviors (e.g., fighting, disagreeableness, inattentiveness), and an inappropriate diagnosis may occur when there is pressure from parents or teachers who wish for their children to be manageable and successful.

Pharmacotherapy for ADHD

For the past 50 years ADHD has been treated with one or another psychomotor stimulant drug. The ability of a stimulant drug such as amphetamine to decrease hyperactivity in children identified as hyperactive or hyperkinetic is viewed as a "paradoxical" effect, because amphetamine generally is known to increase motor activity in children and adults. This unpredicted beneficial effect of amphetamine upon children somewhat disabled by their hyperactivity was revealing; it suggested that the hyperactive/attention deficient/impulsive child has a neurochemical abnormality in the brain that can be relieved temporarily by the pharmacological properties of amphetamine.

The symptoms of ADHD are treated with one or another of a variety of drugs, many of which share common neurochemical effects. Among the stimulant drugs used to treat ADHD, the most frequently prescribed prescribed (for well over half of those diagnosed with ADHD) is methylphenidate (Ritalin). Next in line is dextroamphetamine (Dexedrine), and amphetamine (Adderall), followed by pemoline (Cylert; the utility of pemoline has recently been challenged due to its serious side effects in some children). What do these stimulant drugs have in common?

These drugs share the ability to diminish hyperactivity, improve attention, and decrease impulsivity fairly effectively in the majority (nearly 75%) of those treated, with their effects upon activity generally being greater than their effects upon cognitive processes. In addition, these drugs share the ability to enhance catecholamine neurotransmission broadly by enhancing release and diminishing presynaptic transport (i.e., reuptake) of dopamine, norepinephrine, and (to a lesser extent) serotonin.

Drugs having these amphetamine-like pharmacological properties are not the only ones that have been used successfully to treat ADHD. For example, for those not responding favorably to stimulant drugs, a tricyclic antidepressant drug may likely be prescribed next (e.g., imipramine, desipramine, amitryptaline, nortryptaline, clomipramine).

The utility of such drugs, which generally can inhibit reuptake of norepinephrine and (to a lesser extent) serotonin, suggests that symptoms of ADHD are perhaps attributable to a combined norepinephrine and serotonin dysfunction. The role of serotonin is somewhat unclear, however, given that SSRI pharmacotherapy for ADHD is generally unsuccessful. The child with ADHD who does not respond favorably to a stimulant drug or to a tricyclic antidepressant may be prescribed bupropion (Wellbutrin), a drug that appears to inhibit presynaptic transport of dopamine and norepinephrine (and possibly serotonin).

The newest addition to the pharmacological toolbox for treating ADHD is atomoxetine (Strattera), a drug that relatively selectively inhibits presynaptic transport of norepinephrine. (The FDA has warned of the potential for atomoxetine to produce liver problems or suicidal thoughts.) Another means of enhancing norepinephrine neurotransmission is available in clonidine (Catapres), which activates the alpha-2 subtype of receptor for norepinephrine. Clonidine is sometimes used together with a stimulant drug to minimize the stimulant-induced side effects.

ADHD and the Brain

The clinical effectiveness of drug therapies implicates three neurochemical systems with vast distributions in the brain as having greater or lesser roles in the behavioral and cognitive abnormalities of ADHD: norepinephrine, dopamine, and serotonin (Figures 9.1, 9.2, 11.1). The sites in the brain served by these neurotransmitters that appear to be dysfunctional in ADHD continue to be explored, but data from neuropsychological assessments identifying behavioral and cognitive impairments, together with data from neuroimaging studies, support the following hypothesis (Figure 14.1): A dysfunctional prefrontal cortex (orbitofrontal and dorsolateral cortices), with catecholamine (norepinephrine and dopamine) neurotransmitter projections to subcortical areas of the brain, results in impairments in cognition and movement. Consistent with this hypothesis are findings (in the ADHD brain) of decreased volume of frontal cortex, cerebellum, caudate, putamen, globus pallidus, and corpus callosum (a massive bundle of neurons connecting the right and left cerebral hemispheres).

The involvement of dopamine in this hypothesis is supported by findings from one neuroimaging study showing that the approximately 70%

increase in dopamine presynaptic transport receptors in the brain of ADHD adults can be reduced to normal levels by methylphenidate pharmacotherapy. Methylphenidate (and other stimulant drug) pharmacotherapy is presumed to be successful due to its ability to increase frontal cortical, catecholamine-mediated inhibitory effects upon subcortical (motor) processes, thereby diminishing hyperactivity and impulsivity.

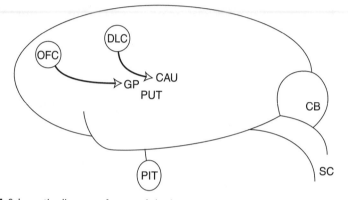

Figure 14.1 Schematic diagram of areas of the brain involved in ADHD. Areas of the cerebral cortex are circled, including: OFC, orbitofrontal cortex; and DLC, dorsolateral cortex. Labeled subcortical areas (CAU, caudate; GP, globus pallidus; PUT, putamen) are richly served by dopamine neurons having axon terminals in the striatum. PIT, pituitary; CB, cerebellum; SC, spinal cord. The lines and arrows represent many catecholamine (norepinephrine and dopamine) neurons projecting from cortex to subcortical structures. This drawing is a view from the side of only the left hemisphere of the brain. The structures identified are represented in each of the two hemispheres.

The apparent involvement of norepinephrine, dopamine, and perhaps serotonin in symptoms of ADHD identifies three neurotransmitters also known to have roles in other psychiatric disorders. This finding is consistent with the rather high rates of comorbidity for ADHD and mood disorders (15–75%) and anxiety (25%). The ADHD child showing comorbidity for mood or anxiety disorders is more likely to benefit from combined drug and behavioral therapies. The fact that pharmacotherapy is the first line of treatment for most other children diagnosed with ADHD is consistent with the fact that no specific environmental risk factors have been identified as contributing to the development of ADHD. Thus, ADHD is characterized as having a strong genetic component, which may or may not require interaction with some degree of psychosocial adversity for the onset of symptoms. The exact nature of the inherited vulnerability in neurochemical processes in the brain is not yet understood.

"So you're telling me, because you're having problems 'handling' Justin in your classroom, that maybe he's got ADHD and maybe we should see a doctor for a prescription drug? But what you're describing is just the behavior of a typical boy! He's energetic, aggressive, quick to get bored with things. Hell, that's in his job description—he's a boy! Maybe his boredom is actually *your* problem! Maybe your class needs to be more challenging to the kids. Justin's grades are fine, so what's the problem? If you're having trouble with a kid who is performing just fine as a student, why give him a prescription drug to mess with his brain? Do your job. They never told you it would be easy. We'll talk to Justin to see if he can be a bit more cooperative, but we won't give him a drug to calm him down. And we won't let some shrink give him a label of ADHD, and then tell us that behavioral therapy doesn't work, so we'll have to medicate Justin. Didn't I just read that maybe 10% of young boys are now getting that label? *Ten percent?* *Ten percent* of American boys need a drug to be normal? There must be sort of conspiracy against boyhood. That should be a violation of the Patriot Act or something! Now, are we finished here?"

The inability to identify interacting environmental and neurochemical causal factors for ADHD means that the selection of therapeutic approaches over the years has been guided largely by the clinical effectiveness of attempted therapeutic techniques, rather than by therapeutic tools that target specific psychosocial or neurochemical factors. The current tendency to select pharmacological treatments rather than behavioral or psychosocial therapies for ADHD is consistent with the findings of clinical investigations. Such studies generally reveal that the labor-intensive behavioral therapeutic approaches are less effective than pharmacotherapeutic approaches, and that combined nondrug and drug therapies are only marginally more successful than pharmacotherapy alone. None of the therapeutic approaches, however, offers enough sustained, trouble-free improvement of ADHD to justify discontinuing the search for the gender-related neurochemical processes in the brain that contribute to the disorder.

Recent findings from neuroimaging studies in humans and from work using animal models of ADHD suggest that there may be abnormalities in the normal differences between the left and right cerebral hemispheres of the brain in ADHD. In other words, the usual laterality of structure and function (Chapter 5) between left side and right side of the frontal cortex and the frontal subcortical areas of the brain (e.g., caudate) may be distorted, missing, or reversed in the ADHD brain. Moreover, these abnormalities of left versus right laterality of structures may be more common or more pronounced in males than in females, a possibility that may provide an explanation of the differences between genders in the incidence of ADHD. Should disturbances in the laterality of brain structure and neurochemical processes be the primary causal factor in ADHD, it will be challenging to find ways in which pharmacotherapy or psychotherapy can affect processes in one side of the brain more so than in the other side of the brain.

Perspective

Pharmacological treatment of ADHD is relatively successful, despite lack of clarity about exactly what is different in the ADHD brain and what is different in the brains of boys, in general, that contributes to the higher incidence of ADHD in boys than in girls. Successful pharmacological treatments identify norepinephrine, dopamine, and serotonin as neurochemical culprits in ADHD; neuroimaging studies of the human brain should further clarify exactly where in the brain these neurochemical abnormalities can be found, and what other neurochemical abnormalities may also be important. The failure to identify psychosocial stressors as factors contributing to ADHD is consistent with the relative ineffectiveness of nonpharmacological treatments. It remains useful to search for nonpharmacological ways to alter brain processes in ADHD, however, because long-term exposure of the young developing brain to a potent stimulant drug is not an ideal remedy.

15

Schizophrenia

Mel knew that so long as he took his medication every day, he would be just fine. But that wasn't so easy to do every day, because he remembered that the pills were originally given to him to poison him so that he would no longer spread God's message. God did speak to him—told him what to do. No one else seemed to hear God's voice, but it was quite real to Mel. Mel had become God's messenger and servant on earth, and this meant certain things had to be said and done, however distasteful; whether or not what Mel did made logical sense to other people did not really matter. For example, burying in his backyard all of the iPods that Mel could steal simply had to be done to diminish the messages Satan sent through the devices. And Mel knew that his iPod gardening fit God's greater plan.

Schizophrenia is a devastating, relapsing psychosis marked by cognitive, emotional, perceptual, and motor disturbances that can present themselves in a variety of forms (i.e., subtypes of psychoses). Over the past century, symptoms of schizophrenia have been labeled and grouped in various ways reflecting reconceptualizations of the nature of the disorder, facilitated by attempts to identify the neurochemical abnormalities in the brain and the environmental factors that cause the illness. Despite great progress in identifying a strong heritability factor for schizophrenia, and some of the environmental stressors that place a person at risk, and discovering drugs that can dramatically improve symptoms of schizophrenia, problems in the brain of a schizophrenic are still not entirely clear.

Clues regarding the neurochemistry of the brain in schizophrenia began appearing in the mid-1950s through observing the effects of several drugs upon behavior. The first clue that schizophrenia might be caused by a disturbance in the neurochemistry of the brain came from two separate but related serendipitous discoveries: The first was the finding that chronic usage of large daily doses of amphetamine could produce a psychosis that was virtually indistinguishable from schizophrenia. The second discovery was that the drug chlorpromazine could improve symptoms of schizophrenia. Neither of these discoveries could, at the time, fully explain the neurochemistry of schizophrenia, because the effects of amphetamine and chlorpromazine on the neurochemistry of the brain were unknown. In the intervening 50-plus years, however, much has been learned in this area.

The study of the pharmacological properties of amphetamine in animals revealed that amphetamine could enhance neurotransmission of dopamine, norepinephrine, and (to a lesser extent) serotonin synapses. It was also discovered that chlorpromazine could prevent dopamine from activating its D2 receptor subtype. These and other findings led to early versions of a dopamine hypothesis for schizophrenia, a theory that continues to evolve and become more complex and neurochemically expansive as research efforts continue to examine the neurochemical factors at play in the schizophrenic brain. More importantly, the knowledge that chlorpromazine improves symptoms of schizophrenia while blocking D2 receptors for dopamine has led to the development of drugs that have pharmacological properties similar to those of chlorpromazine, thereby increasing the options for pharmacotherapeutic alterations of processes in the schizophrenic brain.

Pharmacotherapy for Schizophrenia

The search for more effective and tolerable anti-schizophrenic drugs has produced two groups of antipsychotic medications: older generation (neuroleptic) and newer generation (or atypical) antipsychotics. The older generation antipsychotics are identified in two categories based upon their chemical structures: phenothiazines and butyrophenones. Chlorpromazine (Thorazine) is the original phenothiazine anti-schizophrenic drug. Haloperidol (Haldol) is the most familiar and most widely used butyrophenone. There are literally dozens of phenothiazines and butyrophenones. What do drugs in these two groups of original antipsychotic medications have in common, and what does their clinical effectiveness reveal about the brain of the schizophrenic?

Phenothiazines and butyrophenones share the ability to improve some symptoms of schizophrenia in some schizophrenics. The symptoms that are the more responsive to these drugs came to be called the "positive symptoms" because they are the behavioral abnormalities that showed a positive, beneficial response to neuroleptic drug therapy. These positive symptoms generally include delusions, hallucinations, disorganized speech, and bizarre behavior. The symptoms generally less responsive to older generation antipsychotics, called the "negative symptoms" due to their nonresponsiveness to pharmacotherapy, include flattened emotional response, impoverished speech, diminished initiative and motivation, social withdrawal, lack of feeling pleasure (anhedonia), and intellectual impairment.

Phenothiazines and butyrophenones also share the ability to bind to D2 dopamine receptors and act as antagonists, thereby preventing endogenous dopamine from activating those receptors. Different phenothiazine and butyrophenone drugs bind to D2 receptors to varying degrees, and each of these drugs also alter neurochemical processes other than dopamine. The potency of these drugs for binding to D2 receptors is correlated with the ability of the drugs to improve symptoms of schizophrenia in a clinical setting. This impressive correlation is strong evidence that endogenous dopamine and D2 receptors in the brain are related in some important way to symptoms of schizophrenia, and this fact is among the best evidence supporting a dopamine theory for schizophrenia.

> Hopeless. It seemed hopeless because Ellie never had showed real improvement regardless of the medication they tried. One of the drugs seemed to work, but the bizarre side effects of lip smacking, tongue protrusions, and grimacing were too much to take. They called her a "problem schizophrenic," and that may be why they gave her one of the newer drugs, Clozaril. It helped! She worried about the potential for the drug inducing seizures, as they had warned her, and she did not enjoy the regular examinations checking her out for some other potentially lethal effects, but she felt much better. She felt human again. The drug seemed worth the risks.

The newer generation antipsychotics include a handful of drugs that have come to be used in "problem schizophrenics" who fail to show improvement in response to the older generation antipsychotic drugs. These newer generation drugs have been heralded as advancements because they can be effective in these formerly nonresponsive schizo-phrenics, and because they lack some of the debilitating side effects of the older generation drugs (although they are not without serious risks). These newer generation antipsychotics appear to block multiple subtypes of dopamine receptors (including D1, D2, D3, D4, D5); they are also reported to alter serotonin neurotransmission and to affect several other neurochemicals, including acetylcholine, norepinephrine, and histamine.

One of the newer generation antipsychotics, clozapine (Clozaril), dif-fers in a number of interesting ways from haloperidol, a prototypical older generation antipsychotic: First, clozapine is effective in some schizo-phrenics whose symptoms do not improve on haloperidol. Second, a patient maintained on clozapine is less likely than one using haloperidol to show side effects related to involuntary movements. Third, whereas haloperidol tends to preferentially block D2 receptors in the subcortical caudate and putamen, clozapine tends to block D1, D2, D3, D4, and D5 receptors as well as multiple subtypes of serotonin receptors, and it tends *not* to block receptors for dopamine in the striatum (which could explain its lack of motoric side effects).

The fact that so many of the newer and older generation drugs produce blockade of dopamine receptors, thereby decreasing dopamine neuro-transmission while inhibiting symptoms of schizophrenia, suggests that excessive dopamine neurotransmission might be a neurochemical factor contributing to the onset of schizophrenia. But the fact that the newer generation drugs can have significantly greater potency for altering sero-tonin neurotransmission than for blocking dopamine D2 receptors sug-gests that symptoms of schizophrenia are not likely explained by a dysfunctional dopamine system alone.

Brain Processes and Schizophrenia

Evidence that the brain of a schizophrenic has abnormalities related to dopamine neurotransmission came from some of the very first neu-roimaging studies measuring neurochemistry in the brain of humans (Fig-ure 15.1): Excessive dopamine D2 receptors have been found in various areas of the schizophrenic brain, including the striatum and frontal cor-tex. Moreover, dopamine D1 receptors are deficient in number in the frontal cortex of schizophrenics, and this deficiency is correlated with some of the negative symptoms of schizophrenia. These kinds of findings encouraged further exploration of brain processes in schizophrenics and assessments of the effects of antipsychotic drugs on specific areas of brain.

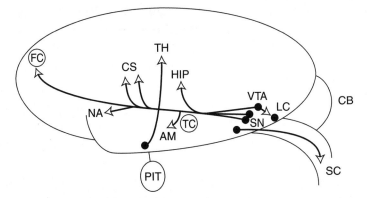

Figure 15.1 Schematic diagram of those portions of dopamine neurons serving areas of the brain involved in schizophrenia. Dopamine neuron cell bodies (black dots) originate in several areas, including the VTA, ventral tegmental area, and SN, substantia nigra. Black lines represent many dopamine axons ending in axon terminals (arrows). Circled areas are sites in the cerebral cortex. Abbreviations: FC, frontal cortex; TC, temporal cortex; TH, thalamus; HIP, hippocampus; AM, amygdala; NA, nucleus accumbens; CS, corpus striatum; LC, locus coeruleus; PIT, pituitary; CB, cerebellum; SC, spinal cord. This drawing is a view from the side of only the left hemisphere of the brain. The structures identified are represented in each of the two hemispheres.

The dopamine D2 abnormality relevant for schizophrenic symptoms appears to be localized in mesolimbic and mesocortical dopamine neurons, which connect the prefrontal cortex with subcortical areas, including the striatum, caudate, putamen, and hippocampus. The prefrontal cortical and limbic (hippocampus) link may represent the key vulnerability for development of schizophrenia, which has long been considered to be a disorder of cognitive (cortical) and emotional (limbic) interactions.

Working within this theoretical framework, the clinical effectiveness of a drug that blocks D2 receptors (e.g., the older generation antipsychotics) is likely due to its direct blockade of D2 receptors in the caudate/putamen; this blockade is presumed to have secondary effects upon the basal ganglia, thalamus, hippocampus, and cortex. In contrast, the newer generation antipsychotic risperidone (Risperdal) can cause greater effects upon dopamine neurotransmission in the frontal cortex and the striatum, and its ability to improve positive *and* negative symptoms may be attributable to its simultaneous alteration of dopamine neurotransmission and blockade of serotonin 5HT-2A receptors in the cortex (Figure 9.2).

Dysfunctional neurochemical processes in these areas of the brain are consistent with other findings from neuroimaging studies. One of the more robust early (1970s) findings of abnormality in the schizophrenic brain is that of enlarged ventricles filled with cerebrospinal fluid. The presence of enlarged ventricles suggests a diminished volume of brain tissue in the brain of schizophrenics, which is supported by more recent (2000s) neuroimaging discoveries of diminished volume of brain tissue and diminished neuronal size in the prefrontal cortex, thalamus, amygdala, and (predominantly) hippocampus in the left hemisphere of the brain (Figure 15.1). Abnormal left–right asymmetry has also been measured in the planum temporale of the temporal cortex (important for integration of auditory and language processes), where the normal left-biased asymmetry in size appears to be reversed in the schizophrenic brain. There are also reports of abnormalities (which can be normalized by clozapine) in blood flow or metabolism in the prefrontal cortex when a schizophrenic is presented with a cognitive task. Finally, abnormalities in blood flow in the temporal cortex have been measured during auditory hallucinations.

In summary, there are numerous documented abnormalities in schizophrenics in areas of the brain known to be involved in emotional, cognitive, and perceptual processes (Figure 15.1). There are also abnormalities in neurochemical processes that are altered by antipsychotic drugs. Not quite enough is known, however, about how neuroanatomical sites and neurochemical processes interact with environmental stressors to contribute to the development of schizophrenia.

Psychotherapy for Schizophrenia

Despite the failure to identify one or more environmental factors that are necessary for the onset of schizophrenia, a variety of environmental stressors have been identified as contributing factors to either the onset of or a relapse of schizophrenia. These include viral infection, drug usage, and emotional climate within the family.

Directing therapy at a potential contributing factor, such as a parent or sibling who is highly emotionally involved with the schizophrenic patient, is not so easily accomplished when the patient's psychosis is in full bloom. It is difficult to converse about a real problem regarding a real parent with a psychotic whose very problem includes inadequate assessment of what is real. Consequently, it is not surprising that pharmacotherapy is essentially required as a first step toward bringing the schizophrenic to an emotional and cognitive state where talk therapy or coping skills training can be understood. Moreover, the fact that antipsychotic drugs rarely normalize *all* symptoms of schizophrenia for a patient, and the fact that as many as 25% of schizophrenics may show no clinically meaningful improvement in response to drug therapy, suggest that non-drug approaches to treatment of schizophrenia will remain useful.

An ideal treatment program would likely include combined pharmacological treatment (offered first), skills training (social and vocational), family psychoeducation (e.g., to minimize the negative impact of a family's negative emotional climate), and community support services (e.g., a paying job). The positive impact of the skills training, family psychoeducation, and community support services would hinge on the ability of pharmacotherapy to first alter the neurochemistry of the brain. This situation marks schizophrenia as relatively unique among psychiatric disorders; its symptoms are so disabling as to render useless most nonpharmacological therapeutic approaches until the neurochemistry of the brain has been sufficiently reorganized to permit the schizophrenic to have constructive social interactions with a therapist.

Gender Differences

There are differences between genders in a variety of characteristics related to schizophrenia: The incidence of schizophrenia is relatively similar for women and men, but women generally exhibit a later age of onset than do men. The later age of onset may be due to the "protective" effects of estrogen, and estrogen may potentiate the therapeutic effectiveness of pharmacotherapy. Women also tend to be less devastated over the long term than do men diagnosed as schizophrenic. For example, women may generally present fewer of the negative symptoms of schizophrenia than do men, and the positive symptoms in women tend to show a more favorable response to pharmacotherapy than they do in men. This combination of factors permits a better quality of life for the female schizophrenic than for the male schizophrenic. But not all of the gender differences are good news for women—women are more likely than men to experience one of the devastating side effects involving involuntary movements (i.e., tardive dyskinesia) that can be induced by the therapeutic use of D2 antagonist drugs. These differences between genders are likely to be partially explained by differences in brain and physiology between women and men, but current knowledge about brain processes in schizophrenia do not yet provide an explanation.

Perspective

Knowledge about the abnormalities in the brains of schizophrenics has accumulated over 50 years, benefiting from a wide variety of studies: serendipitous findings and controlled experimental trials in clinical settings, research on brain neurochemistry in animal models of schizophrenia, and neuroimaging of the human brain. The findings have led to a neurochemical theory of schizophrenia that, with the neurotransmitter dopamine as its focal point, continues to evolve and become more complex neurochemically. This evolving theory represents a triumph of biomedical research for its demonstration of the disordered functioning of brain sites, endogenous neurochemicals, and receptors in synapses in a spectacularly disabling psychological disorder. Indeed, the study of the schizophrenic brain is often made the poster story of contemporary behavioral neuroscience, despite the fact that much remains mysterious about the brain of a schizophrenic. The fact that there remains some mystery about the causes of schizophrenia, the precise neurochemical abnormalities in the schizophrenic brain, gender differences, and how to help schizophrenics who fail to respond to all current therapies, makes clear that the wondrous complexity of the human brain and its relation to behavior is not entirely understood. There is still plenty of work to be found here!

Annotated Bibliography for Part III

Neurobiology of Mental Illness—Second Edition. Charney, Dennis S., & Nestler, Eric J. New York: Oxford University Press, 2004.
The chapters in this reference volume review neurobiological issues related to psychological disorders, with a heavy emphasis upon brain neurochemistry and pharmacotherapy. Although it is difficult to find the word *psychotherapy* in this volume, it is nonetheless valuable, if challenging, reading. In fact, you might

consider reading Feldman and Quenzer's *Psychopharmacology* (in bibliography for Part II) prior to taking on chapters in this volume.

Textbook of Psychopharmacology—Third Edition. Schatzberg, Alan F., & Nemeroff, Charles B. Arlington, VA: American Psychiatric Association, 2004.
The chapters in this volume review all you could hope to know about drugs used to treat various psychological disorders. In addition, there are some very helpful chapters introducing (at an intermediate level) the reader to principles of pharmacology and synaptic neurotransmission.

The Neuroscience of Psychotherapy. Cozolino, Louis. New York: Norton, 2002.
This book offers bold speculations concerning how psychotherapy may be reorganizing brain processes.

Physiology of Behavior—Eighth Edition. Carlson, Neil R. Boston: Allyn & Bacon, 2003.
Many textbooks focus upon the relation of brain to behavior. This one is particularly good at revealing the relation between basic research using animals as subjects and learning about the human brain and behavior. This book is a readable and perceptive survey of the study of brain and behavior, and it touches upon a number of psychological disorders.

PART IV
CONCLUDING PERSPECTIVE

16

Probing a Frontier

Frank's psychiatrist told him, "Well, I don't know that venlafaxine will help you feel any better, but I sure do hope so." This did not sound much like a vote of confidence, so Frank asked his psychiatrist why he seemed uncertain about the potential outcome.

"Well, Frank, we didn't exactly know why the fluoxetine relieved your obsessive–compulsive disorder 6 years ago, and we don't know why it stopped being helpful to you now. So we'll try a different drug now and see what happens."

Hearing that, Frank then repeated what his psychiatrist had explained to him long ago: that fluoxetine and other SSRIs alter serotonin levels in the brain and that's why they relieved Frank's OCD; Frank didn't know much, but he knew that much, and he thought his psychiatrist should know it also.

"Sure, that's the story we tell, Frank—that SSRIs enhance serotonin function in the brain, and so we *presume* that's why symptoms of OCD improve—but that's only a reasonable guess. We know a lot less about why our therapies work than you think. And we know a lot less about the chemistry of your obsessed brain than you think, Frank. Just because you pay me a lot of money for my advice and my prescriptions doesn't mean I actually know exactly what I am doing! If I prescribe a drug for you and it helps, I'm pleased—and I'm also relieved."

Studying the brain, we might as well be studying Mars. On a clear night, when the astronomical and atmospheric situation permits, we can see Mars from our seat on the swing on the front porch. Aided by a telescope, we can see its colors and more prominent features. Shoot up a rocket and land a probe, we can photograph peaks, valleys, rocks, and dust, and we can attempt to measure a few familiar substances such as water and oxygen. But after all that, we still don't know much about Mars. We don't know nearly enough to teach all that we'd wish to teach about that frontier.

Brain as Frontier

Mars is no more of a frontier for exploration than is the brain, despite the brain's proximity within the nearest skull. The brain reveals almost nothing of its structure and function as we look at it with our naked eye. But when we cut it up, treat it with chemicals, and then explore it with microscopes, we can learn some things about the brain's structure and chemicals. But we can't learn all things about structure and chemistry, because we are limited to looking for those things that we already surmise may be there—those things that we have the technology to actually measure. You cannot measure what you do *not* know is there!

After identififying some structures and chemicals, we cannot merely guess or imagine their functions. We need to actively manipulate and measure those structures and chemicals to learn about their functions. And to study the behavioral functions of structures and chemicals in the brain, we need to make those manipulations and measurements in living, awake, behaving humans or animals, because only the living behave. Conducting such research is a difficult business: The measurements and manipulations that can be made in humans as well as animals are limited by available technologies and by ethical issues. More importantly, studies of the relation among brain structures, chemicals, and behavioral functions are limited to those structures and chemicals that have been previously identified as measurable and manipulable.

How many times have the neurochemicals dopamine, serotonin, and norepinephrine proved to be important for dysfunctional behaviors ranging from depression to anxiety to overeating to ADHD to psychosis? Dopamine, serotonin, and norepinephrine—over and over again we've read of their relevance. Why? In part, because the first developed techniques for detecting the presence of neurochemicals in the brain were techniques for measuring *those particular neurochemicals*. And if you can detect them, then you can study them. If you can find them in specific places in the brain, and if chemists can provide agonist and antagonist drugs for activating or blocking the receptors for those neurotransmitters, then you can use those drugs to manipulate those neurochemical processes in the synapses by conducting experiments intended to learn about the functions of the neurochemicals in those brain sites. In short, the availability of tools for measurement and for manipulation provokes research activity focused upon those processes that are currently capable of being manipulated, not because they are necessarily the more important processes, but because they can be studied more readily than other, perhaps equally important, processes.

So we've learned a lot about dopamine, serotonin and norepinephrine because we've studied them very much. And because the brain is not organized in a way that simply assigns single chemicals or single sites to single functions, we find that a system of dopamine (or serotonin or norepinephrine) neurons appears to be involved in a wide range of normal behaviors *and* in a wide range of dysfunctional behaviors. This knowledge does not assure us that dopamine is *the* major player for these functions, nor does it assure us that the specific sites in which dopamine is found are the only brain sites involved in these functions. Other neurochemicals in other sites in the brain, unidentified or merely measured and manipulated less often in experiments, may also be major players in these same functions. We just won't know until we study them as intensively as we've studied dopamine (or serotonin or norepinephrine).

Identifying unknown processes in the brain depends upon the invention of new technologies, and so does the study of the relation between brain processes and functions. Despite recent magnificent technological advances and the use of these new identification and measurement tools (e.g., neuroimaging), it is safe to say that we know much less than half of what the brain is and how the brain does what it does. We certainly don't know enough about the brain to build another functional one. And we don't know enough about the brain to fix it properly when dysfunctional behaviors suggest that the brain is broken. We can tinker with it pharmacologically, we can make some adjustments psychotherapeutically, but we cannot restore the brain to its original condition; we can only patch it up and hope that it remains functional for a while.

Areas of Ignorance

What more do we need to know to improve our abilities to patch up dysfunctional processes in the brain and nervous system? We ultimately need to know the identity of all of the neurochemicals in the brain and the relation among sites and neurochemical systems that are involved in psychological processes and behavior. While we patiently wait for all of that information to be revealed, we need to learn all that we can about identifiable, measurable abnormalities in the brains of people diagnosed with disorders, including those patients who fail to respond to drugs (or psychotherapy) that do help the many other patients diagnosed with the same disorder. We also need to know more about the differences between men and women in the structure and functions of sites and neurochemicals in the brain—differences that are important for normal and dysfunctional behaviors. A better understanding of these gender-related differences in the brain should allow us to develop better gender-related options for therapy.

A similar point can be made for the need to know more about how the "same" disorders in children, adults, and the elderly are different, so that therapeutic interventions can be tailored to best address the neurochemical, psychological, and social needs of patients in very different phases of life. We also need to know much more about how environmental or social stressors interact with neurochemical or physiological vulnerabilities to affect the brain and nervous system and cause the onset of dysfunction. We also need to know more about how inherited, genetic predispositions establish neurochemical or physiological vulnerabilities to specific dysfunctions, and how these genetic vulnerabilities permit environmental or social stressors to cause specific psychopathology. We need to know more about how successful pharmacotherapy and psychotherapy alter the brain and nervous system, and whether or not effective pharmacotherapy or psychotherapy alters the same or different neurochemical processes. And we need to know more about whether or not these therapies differentially affect the developing brain versus the adult brain.

Although we may not know much, we *do* know enough to make improvements in the lives of humans who are suffering disabling brain and behavioral disorders. How have we come to know even that much about the relation between a dysfunctional brain and the resulting dysfunctional behavior?

Pharmacology as a Tool

Dysfunctional behavior is first and foremost an important problem for the person who is suffering and for his or her therapist, whereas it is merely an interesting phenomenon for study for the behavioral scientist or neurobiologist. Given the top priority of helping the psychologicially disabled patient, clinicians are likely to use whatever therapy is effective (and relatively safe)—drug or talk—to improve the patient's quality of life. And more often than not, there is a drug with demonstrated effectiveness for a particular disorder.

The clinical effectiveness of drugs has led the way toward understanding the relation between dysfunctional brain functioning and behavior: When a drug therapy improves behavioral symptoms of a disorder, even when it is not known what the drug is doing to brain neurochemistry, it is assumed that the drug is changing behavior by acting upon a neurochemical process(es) that causes the symptoms. This situation provides an opportunity for investigating aspects of etiology or aspects of ongoing disordered neurochemistry related to symptoms. The opportunity can be pursued in several ways. First, the drug with clinical effectiveness can be studied to determine its mechanism of action—how it affects neurochemistry, receptors in synapses, and systems of neurons in sites in the brain. This type of study is best conducted in animals in order to take advantage of technical approaches that cannot be used in humans. Second, the drug with clinical effectiveness can be studied in a more limited way in humans, sometimes using neuroimaging techniques to measure how and where the drug is acting in the brain. Most of what we know about the relation between dysfunctional brain functioning and behavior has come from the opportunities presented by the clinical effectiveness of pharmacotherapy. These opportunities can guide our course when probing within the brain by suggesting the structures and chemicals to manipulate or to measure.

Diagnostic Categories as Help and Hindrance

Systematic research exploring the relation between processes in the brain and symptoms of behavioral disorders requires definitions of disorders. If two scientists in two different clinical research settings are going to study the neurochemistry of schizophrenia, and they want their results to be compared in a meaningful way, they must agree upon the signs and symptoms that identify a person with schizophrenia. The DSM provides a framework for defining disorders that is useful for making diagnoses— that is, to assign people with various symptoms to specific categories and subcategories of illness. Such classification schemes (like any operational definition in science) represent attempts to be somewhat precise in what is being defined (e.g., *schizophrenia*), but these classification schemes are somewhat arbitrary. For example, the DSM uses behavioral symptoms as the data for classification/diagnosis. The DSM does not use etiology or causes of disorders as data for classification/diagnosis, although such data can be useful for distinguishing among different disorders. The important issue here is to determine whether the DSM is constructed in such a way that different categories (e.g., depression, anxiety, schizophrenia, anorexia) and subcategories represent meaningful and useful ways to separate people who have distinctly different brain and behavioral problems?

Actually, there might be a better way to categorize people with disorders. In fact, when considering the high rates of comorbidity for the various DSM categories, we might ask whether this extensive comorbidity reveals some sloppiness in our diagnostic categories. In the short form: There is considerable overlap in the categories. Some people labeled depressed also show anxiety; some people labeled with anxiety also show depression; some people labeled bulimic also show depression, etc. Further evidence of this problem with categories can be found in pharmacotherapy: an "antidepressant" drug may be effective for treating bulimia or anxiety; an "antipsychotic" drug may be effective for treating bipolar disorder. What does it tell us about the disorders if the same drug can be used to treat them? Does it tell us that the different categories of disorder have common underlying neurochemical abnormalities? If so, then these categories seem not so very distinct after all. Does it tell us that our classification scheme is unwittingly mixing (into a single label) different brain–behavioral problems? To tackle this issue, perhaps revised classification schemes should use a greater variety of data (than simply behavioral symptoms) to delineate categories of illness. Newer classification schemes could use behavioral symptoms *and* neuroimaging assessments of the brain *and* genetic information *and* physiological or behavioral responses to probes (e.g., administration of a drug, assignment of a cognitive task) together to create more sharply defined diagnostic categories and subcategories of brain and behavioral disorders.

Just as a revised paradigm for classification and diagnosis would be useful to facilitate study of the etiology of disorders (and ultimately to improve therapy), so too might it be useful to have a revised paradigm for study of the relation between brain neurochemistry and behavior. Should the neurochemistry of the synapse continue to be the focal point for understanding the relation between brain chemistry and behavior?

Synapse as Frame of Reference

For several decades the synapse and synaptic receptors have provided a conceptual framework that has dominated the study of psychopharmacology and the study of the relation between brain neurochemistry and behavior. The working assumption has been that a psychoactive drug (or an endogenous neurochemical) has its effects upon behavior and psychological processes by directly (or indirectly) altering the functioning of receptors in synapses. That paradigm has served very well to guide research activities that have expanded our understanding of brain processes related to behaviors. Theories of various behavioral disorders that attempt to link synaptic, receptor-mediated processes to behavioral symptoms are discussed in the chapters of Part III of this book.

But that conceptual framework may need to be expanded because it is now known that the presynaptic neurotransmitter, interacting with postsynaptic receptors, has consequences for intraneuronal biochemical processes in the postsynaptic neuron that are important for understanding the relation between brain chemistry and behavior. These postsynaptic intraneuronal processes are rarely mentioned in this book, because relatively little is known about their roles in behavior, and because the most useful point of reference for brain scientists thinking about the relation between brain processes and behavior has been the synapse. This focus will likely be expanded to incorporate these intracellular chemical processes as well as synaptic, receptor processes. Such a revised paradigm should expand the list of potential neurochemical targets for new therapeutic drugs.

Tools for Research

Synaptic and intracellular neurochemical processes will continue to be targets for neuroimaging techniques applied to the human brain. Some of the limitations and technical constraints imposed upon neuroimaging clinical studies are likely to be overcome to facilitate longitudinal analysis of brain and behavioral disorders. Longitudinal neuroimaging studies will be necessary to learn if and when specific neuroanatomical and neurochemical abnormalities appear (1) prior to the onset of a disorder, (2) during florid display of symptoms, or (3) during therapeutic-induced diminishment of symptoms. These kinds of longitudinal studies are difficult and expensive, but they are important for determining which areas of the human brain and which neurochemicals interact to constitute the system of brain processes relevant for the development of a specific behavioral disorder. Understanding how multiple sites and various neurochemicals in the brain function within a system of neurons should be greatly facilitated by the application of neuroimaging techniques to investigations of behavioral responses to experimental tasks or challenges.

In addition, the strategies and techniques of molecular genetics and behavioral genetics will provide new information regarding the multiple interacting factors that determine the vulnerability for development of a specific brain and behavioral disorder. These studies of inherited vulnerability factors, however, will continue to contribute to the tendency of some brain scientists to "reduce" behavioral and psychological disorders to genetics and underlying neurochemical processes. This kind of reductionism is not new, but it is a continuing nuisance, because it attempts to diminish the demonstrated importance of environmental and social factors for etiology. More importantly, that bias tends to devalue nondrug, nonphysiological therapeutic approaches for treatment.

New Therapeutic Approaches

A few psychotherapeutic approaches have been shown to alter neurochemical processes in the brain, but very little research has been done to measure which psychotherapeutic interventions are effective for altering brain processes for specific behavioral disorders, because these kinds of studies are very difficult to conduct. Such research will be facilitated by the continuing development of neuroimaging techniques. This work should illuminate whether drugs or talk complement or duplicate one another in the neurochemical mechanisms by which they improve symptoms. This information should help us to learn how these two therapeutic approaches can be better used in combination in the clinical setting.

The clinical treatment of dysfunctional behavior should also benefit from the development of new drugs that are neuroanatomically and neurochemically more selective. Drugs that can preferentially target specific subsets of (e.g., dopamine) synapses in specific areas of brain and also target specific subtypes of receptors (or intracellular chemical processes) generally relieve symptoms better with fewer risks of side effects. Moreover, drugs that can alter processes in a relatively selective manner but do so across multiple neurochemical systems (e.g., a drug that is both a dopamine D2 antagonist as well as a serotonin 5HT-1A agonist) should bring similar advantages for pharmacotherapy.

The traditional categories of pharmacotherapy and psychotherapy may also be complemented increasingly by surgical approaches such as transplanting fetal tissue or stem cells into specific regions of brain, and approaches such as transcranial magnetic stimulation of brain or vagal nerve stimulation.

Finally, basic research in animals and humans that provides greater understanding of the brain processes related to normal as well as disordered behaviors ultimately will improve the options for clinical treatment. Combining the advantages of newer, more selective drugs with (1) nonpharmacological techniques for manipulating the brain and nervous system, (2) psychotherapeutic techniques known to target specific neurochemical processes, and (3) psychosocial therapeutic techniques that target a patient's relationships with family members and peers should create treatment programs that are more effective for improving the quality of life for people suffering from disordered brain processes and dysfunctional behaviors.

References

Agras, W. S. (2004). Treatment of eating disorders. In A. F. Schatzberg & C. B. Nemeroff (Eds.), *Textbook of Psychopharmacology*, Second Edition (pp. 1031–1040). Washington, DC: American Psychiatric Press.

Agras, W. S., Rossiter, E. M., Arnow, B., Schneider, J. A., Telch, C. F., Raeburn, S. D., Bruce, B., Perl, M. & Koran, L. M. (1992). Pharmacologic and cognitive-behavioral treatment for bulimia nervosa: A controlled comparison. *American Journal of Psychiatry 149*: 82–87.

American Psychiatric Association (2004). Practice guidelines for the treatment of patients with schizophrenia, Second Edition. *American Journal of Psychiatry 161*(2): 1–56.

—— (2002). Practice guidelines for the treatment of patients with bipolar disorder (Revision). *American Journal of Psychiatry 159*(4): 1–50.

—— (2000). *Diagnostic and Statistical Manual of Mental Disorders*, Fourth Edition. Washington, DC: American Psychiatric Press.

—— (2000). Practice guidelines for the treatment of patients with eating disorders (Revision). *American Journal of Psychiatry 157*(1): 1–39.

—— (2000). Practice guidelines for the treatment of patients with major depressive disorder (Revision). *American Journal of Psychiatry 157*(4): 1–45.

—— (1995). Practice guidelines for the treatment of patients with substance use disorders: Alcohol, cocaine, opinoids. *American Journal of Psychiatry 152*(11): 1–59.

Anderson, S. L., & Teicher, M. H. (2000). Sex differences in dopamine receptors and their relevance to ADHD. *Neuroscience and Biobehavioral Reviews 24*: 137–141.

Ball, G. G. (1974). Vagotomy: Effect on electrically elicited eating and self-stimulation in the lateral hypothalamus. *Science 184*: 484–485.

Barlow, D. H., & Raffa, S. D. (2002). Psychosocial treatments for panic disorders, phobias, and generalized anxiety disorder. In P. E. Nathan & J. M. Gorman (Eds.), *A Guide to Treatments That Work*, Second Edition (pp. 301–335). New York: Oxford.

Berman, K. F., & Meyer-Lindenberg, A. (2004). Functional brain imaging studies in schizophrenia. In D. S. Charney & E. J. Nestler (Eds.), *Neurobiology of Mental Illness*, Second Edition (pp. 311–323). New York: Oxford.

Berthoud, H.-R. (2004). Neural control of appetite: Cross-talk between homeostatic and non-homeostatic systems. *Appetite 43*: 315–317.

Biver, F., Lotstra, F., Monclus, M., Wikler, D., Damhaut, P., Mendlewicz, J. & Goldman, S. (1996). Sex difference in 5HT2 receptor in the living human brain. *Neuroscience Letters 204*: 25–28.

Blood, A. J., & Zatorre, R. J. (2001). Intensely pleasurable responses to music correlate with activity in brain regions implicated in reward and emotion. *Proceedings of the National Academy of Sciences 98*: 11818–11823.

Blundell, J. E., & Finlayson, G. (2004). Is susceptibility to weight gain characterized by homeostatic or hedonic risk factors for overconsumption? *Physiology and Behavior 82*: 21–25.

Boland, R. J., & Keller, M. B. (2004). Diagnostic classification of mood disorders: Historical context and implications for neurobiology. In D. S. Charney, & E. J. Nestler (Eds.), *Neurobiology of Mental Illness*, Second Edition (pp. 357–368). New York: Oxford.

Bradford, D., Stroup, S., & Lieberman, J. (2002). Pharmacological treatments for schizophrenia. In P. E. Nathan & J. M. Gorman (Eds.), *A Guide to Treatments That Work*, Second Edition (pp. 169–199). New York: Oxford.

Bray, G. A., & Tartaglia, L. A. (2000). Medicinal strategies in the treatment of obesity. *Nature 404*: 672–677.

Bremner, J. D. (2005). *Brain Imaging Handbook*. New York: Norton.

Campfield, L. A., Smith, F. J., & Burn, P. (1998). Strategies and potential molecular targets for obesity treatment. *Science 280*: 1383–1387.

Chambless, D. L., & Ollendick, T. H. (2001). Empirically supported psychological interventions: Controversies and evidence. *Annual Review of Psychology 52*: 685–716.

Chang, L., Ernst, T., Strickland, T., & Mehringer, C. M. (1999). Gender effects on persistent cerebral metabolite changes in the frontal lobes of abstinent cocaine users. *American Journal of Psychiatry 156*: 716–722.

Charney, D. S., & Bremner, J. D. (2004). The neurobiology of anxiety disorders. In D. S. Charney & E. J. Nestler (Eds.), *Neurobiology of Mental Illness*, Second Edition (pp. 605–627). New York: Oxford.

References

Cho, R. Y., Gilbert, A., & Lewis, D. A. (2004). The neurobiology of schizophrenia. In D. S. Charney & E. J. Nestler (Eds.), *Neurobiology of Mental Illness*, Second Edition (pp. 299–310). New York: Oxford.

Craighead, W. E., Hart, A. B., Craighead, L. W., & Ilardi, S. S. (2002). Psychosocial treatments for major depressive disorder. In P. E. Nathan & J. M. Gorman (Eds.), *A Guide to Treatments That Work,* Second Edition (pp. 245–261). New York: Oxford.

Craighead, W. E., Miklowitz, D., Frank, E. & Vajk, F. C. (2002). Psychosocial treatments for bipolar disorder. In P. E. Nathan & J. M. Gorman (Eds.), *A Guide to Treatments That Work*, Second Edition (pp. 263–275). New York: Oxford.

Cyranowski, J. M., Frank, E., Young, E., & Shear, M. K. (2000). Adolescent onset of the gender difference in lifetime rates of major depression: A theoretical model. *Archives of General Psychiatry 57*: 21–27.

Damsma, G., Pfaus, J. G., Wenkstern, D., Phillips, A. G. & Fibiger, H. C. (1992). Sexual behavior increases dopamine transmission in the nucleus accumbens and striatum of male rats: Comparison with novelty and locomotion. *Behavioral Neuroscience 106*: 181–191.

Davis, M. (2004). Functional neuroanatomy of anxiety and fear. In D. S. Charney & E. J. Nestler (Eds.), *Neurobiology of Mental Illness*, Second Edition (pp. 584–604). New York: Oxford.

DeRubeis, R. J., & Crits-Christoph, P. (1998). Empirically supported individual and group psychological treatments for adult mental disorders. *Journal of Consulting and Clinical Psychology 66*: 37–52.

Dougherty, D. D., Rauch, S. L., & Jenike, M. A. (2002). Pharmacological treatments for obsessive compulsive disorder. In P. E. Nathan & J. M. Gorman (Eds.), *A Guide to Treatments That Work*, Second Edition (pp. 387–410). New York: Oxford.

Drevets, W. C., Gadde, K. M., & Krishnan, K. R. R. (2004). Neuroimaging studies of mood disorders. In D. S. Charney & E. J. Nestler (Eds.), *Neurobiology of Mental Illness*, Second Edition (pp. 461–490). New York: Oxford.

Duman, R. S. (2004). The neurochemistry of depressive disorders: Preclinical studies. In D. S. Charney & E. J. Nestler (Eds.), *Neurobiology of Mental Illness*, Second Edition (pp. 421–439). New York: Oxford.

Epping-Jordan, M. P., Watkins, S. S., Koob, G. F., & Markou, A. (1998). Dramatic decreases in brain reward function during nicotine withdrawal. *Nature 393*: 76–79.

Faraone, S. V., & Biederman, J. (2004). Neurobiology of attention deficit hyperactivity disorder. In D. S. Charney & E. J. Nestler (Eds.), *Neurobiology of Mental Illness*, Second Edition (pp. 979–999). New York: Oxford.

Finney, J. W. & Moos, R. H. (2002). Psychosocial treatments for alcohol use disorders. In P. E. Nathan & J. M. Gorman (Eds.), *A Guide to Treatments That Work*, Second Edition (pp. 157–168). New York: Oxford.

Fowler, J. S., & Volkow, N. D. (2004). Neuroimaging in substance abuse research. In D. S. Charney & E. J. Nestler (Eds.), *Neurobiology of Mental Illness*, Second Edition (pp. 740–752). New York: Oxford.

Frezza, M., Di Padova, C., Pozzato, G., Terpin, M., Baraona, E., & Lieber, C. S. (1990). High blood alcohol levels in women: The role of decreased gastric alcohol dehydrogense activity and first-pass metabolism. *The New England Journal of Medicine 322*: 95–99.

Geracioti, T. D., & Liddle, R. A. (1988). Impaired cholecystokinin secretion in bulimia nervosa. *New England Journal of Medicine 319*: 683–688.

Giantonio, G. W., Lund, N. L., & Gerall, A. A. (1970). Effect of diencephalic and rhinencephalic lesions on the male rat's sexual behavior. *Journal of Comparative and Physiological Psychology 73*: 38–46.

Gibbs, J., Young, R. C., & Smith, G. P. (1973). Cholecystokinin decreases food intake in rats. *Journal of Comparative and Physiological Psychology 84*: 488–495.

Goddard, A. W., Coplan, J. D., Shekhar, A., Gorman, J. M., & Charney, D. S. (2004). In D. S. Charney & E. J. Nestler (Eds.), *Neurobiology of Mental Illness*, Second Edition (pp. 661–679). New York: Oxford.

Goldapple, K., Segal, Z., Garson, C., Lau, M., Bieling, P., Kennedy, S., & Mayberg, H. (2004). Modulation of cortical-limbic pathways in major depression. *Archives of General Psychiatry 61*: 34–41.

Goldbloom, D. S., & Olmsted, M. P. (1993). Pharmacotherapy of bulimia nervosa with fluoxetine: Assessment of clinically significant attitudinal change. *American Journal of Psychiatry 150*: 770–774.

Greenhill, L. L., & Ford, R. E. (2002). Childhood attention-deficit hyperactivity disorder: Pharmacological treatments. In P. E. Nathan & J. M. Gorman (Eds.), *A Guide to Treatments That Work*, Second Edition (pp. 25–55). New York: Oxford.

Hammer, R. P. (1984). The sexually dimorphic region of the preoptic area in rats contains denser opiate receptor binding sites in females. *Brain Research 308*: 172–176.

Havel, P. J. (2001). Peripheral signals conveying metabolic information to the brain: Short-term and long-term regulation of food intake and energy homeostasis. *Experimental Biology and Medicine 226*: 963–977.

Hernandez, L.. & Hoebel, B. G. (1988). Food reward and cocaine increase extracellular dopamine in the nucleus accumbens as measured by microdialysis. *Life Sciences 42*: 1705–1712.

References

Hinshaw, S. P., Klein, R. G., & Abikoff, H. B. (2002). Childhood attention-deficit hyperactivity disorder: Nonpharmacological treatments and their combination with medication. In P. E. Nathan & J. M. Gorman (Eds.), *A Guide to Treatments That Work*, Second Edition (pp. 3–23). New York: Oxford.

Hsu, L. K. (1986). The treatment of anorexia nervosa. *American Journal of Psychiatry 143*: 573–581.

Hughes, J. R. &. Bickel, W. K. (1997). Modeling drug dependence behaviors for animal and human studies. *Pharmacology Biochemistry and Behavior 57*: 413–417.

Hurt, R. D., Sachs, D. P. L., Glover, E. D., Offord, K. P., Johnston, J. A., Dale, L. C., Khayrallah, M. A., Schroeder, D. R., Glover, P. N., Sullivan, C. R., Croghan, I. T., & Sullivan, P. M. (1997). A comparison of sustained-release bupropion and placebo for smoking cessation. *New England Journal of Medicine 337*: 1195–1202.

Kaye, W., Strober, M., & Jimerson, D. (2004). The neurobiology of eating disorders. In D. S. Charney & E. J. Nestler (Eds.), *Neurobiology of Mental Illness*, Second Edition (pp. 1112–1128). New York: Oxford.

Keck, P. E., & McElroy, S. L. (2002). Pharmacological treatments for bipolar disorder. In P. E. Nathan & J. M. Gorman (Eds.), *A Guide to Treatments That Work*, Second Edition (pp. 277–299). New York: Oxford.

Kelsey, D., Wernicke, J., Trapp, N. J., & Harder, D. (2002). Once-daily atomoxetine treatment for children and adolescents with attention deficit hyperactivity disorder: A randomized, placebo-controlled study. *American Journal of Psychiatry 159*: 1896–1901.

Kent, J. M., & Rauch, S. L. (2004). Neuroimaging studies of anxiety disorders. In D. S. Charney & E. J. Nestler (Eds.), *Neurobiology of Mental Illness*, Second Edition (pp. 639–660). New York: Oxford.

Klein, D. A., & Walsh, B. T. (2004). Eating disorders: Clinical features and pathophysiology. *Physiology and Behavior 81*: 359–374.

Kopelowicz, A., Liberman, R. P., & Zarate, R. (2002). Psychosocial treatments for schizophrenia. In P. E. Nathan & J. M. Gorman (Eds.), *A Guide to Treatments That Work*, Second Edition (pp. 201–228). New York: Oxford.

Kraly, F. S. (1990). Drinking elicited by eating. *Progress in Psychobiology and Physiological Psychology 14*: 67–133.

Krystal, J. H., Abi-Dargham, A., Laruelle, M., & Moghaddam, B. (2004). Pharmacological models of psychoses. In D. S. Charney & E. J. Nestler (Eds.), *Neurobiology of Mental Illness*, Second Edition (pp. 287–298). New York: Oxford.

Lehmann, H. E., & Ban, T. A. (1997). The history of the psychopharmacology of schizophrenia. *Canadian Journal of Psychiatry 42*: 152–163.

Leshner, A. I. (1997). Addiction is a brain disease, and it matters. *Science 278*: 45–47.

Leuchter, A. F., Cook, I. A., Witte, E. A., Morgan, M., & Abrams, M. (2002). Changes in brain function of depressed subjects during treatment with placebo. *American Journal of Psychiatry 159*: 122–129.

LeVay, S. (1991). A difference in hypothalamic structure between heterosexual and homosexual men. *Science 253*: 1034–1037.

Lingford-Hughes, A. R., Gacinovic, S., Boddington, S. J., Costa, D. C., Pilowsky, L. S., Ell, P. J., Marshall, E. J., & Kerwin, R. W. (2000). Levels of gamma-aminobutyric acid-benzodiazepine receptors in abstinent, alcohol-dependent women: Preliminary findings from an 123I-iomazenil single photon emission tomography study. *Alcoholism: Clinical and Experimental Research 24*: 1449–1455.

Little, K. Y., Patel, U. N., Clark, T. B., & Butts, J. D. (1996). Alteration of brain dopamine and serotonin levels in cocaine users: A preliminary report. *American Journal of Psychiatry 153*: 1216–1218.

Mann, J. J. & Arango, V. (2004). Abnormalities of brain structure and function in mood disorders based upon postmortem investigations. In D. S. Charney & E. J. Nestler (Eds.), *Neurobiology of Mental Illness*, Second Edition (pp. 512–522). New York: Oxford.

McEwen, B. S., Lieberberg, I., Chaptal, C., & Krey, L. C. (1977). Aromatizatiton: Important for sexual differentiation of the neonatal rat brain. *Hormones and Behavior 9*: 249–263.

McHugh, P. R., & Slavney, P. R. (1998). *The Perspectives of Psychiatry*, Second Edition. Baltimore: Johns Hopkins University Press.

Moran, T. H. (2004). Gut peptides in the control of food intake: 30 years of ideas. *Physiology and Behavior 82*: 175–180.

Moran, T. H., Ameglio, P. J., Peyton, H. J., Schwartz, G. J., & McHugh, P. R. (1993). Blockade of type A, but not type B, CCK receptors postpones satiety in rhesus monkeys. *American Journal of Physiology 265*: R620–R624.

Moran, T. H., & Kinzig, K. P. (2004). Gastrointestinal satiety signals II. Cholecystokinin. *American Journal of Physiology 286*: G183–G188.

Nemeroff, C. B. &, Schatzberg, A. F. (2002). Pharmacological treatments for unipolar depression. In P. E. Nathan & J. M. Gorman (Eds.), *A Guide to Treatments That Work*, Second Edition (pp. 229–243). New York: Oxford.

O'Brien, C. P., & Cornish, J. W. (2004). Principles of the pharmacotherapy of substance abuse disorders. In D. S. Charney & E. J. Nestler (Eds.), *Neurobiology of Mental Illness*, Second Edition (pp. 753–765). New York: Oxford.

O'Brien, C. P., & McKay, J. (2002). Pharmacological treatments for substance use disorders. In P. E. Nathan & J. M. Gorman (Eds.), *A Guide to Treatments That Work*, Second Edition (pp. 125–156). New York: Oxford.

References

Okubo, Y., Suhara, T., Suzuki, K., Kobayashi, K., Inoue, O., Terasaki, O., Someya, Y., Sassa, T., Sudo, Y., Matsushima, E., Iyo, M., Tateno, Y., & Toru, M. (1997). Decreased prefrontal dopamine D1 receptors in schizophrenia revealed by PET. *Nature 385*: 634–636.

Olds, J., & Milner, P. (1954). Positive reinforcement produced by electrical stimulation of septal area and other regions of rat brain. *Journal of Comparative and Physiological Psychology 47*: 419–427.

O'Malley, S. S., Jaffe, A. J., Rode, S., & Rounsaville, B. J. (1996). Experience of a "slip" among alcoholics treated with naltrexone or placebo. *American Journal of Psychiatry 153*: 281–283.

Oswald, L. M., & Wand, G. S. (2004). Opioids and alcoholism. *Physiology and Behavior 81*: 339–358.

Pagnoni, G., & Berns, G. S. (2004). Brain Imaging in Psychopharmacology. In A. F. Schatzberg & C. B. Nemeroff (Eds.), *Textbook of Psychopharmacology*, Second Edition (pp. 163–172). Washington, DC: American Psychiatric Press.

Payne, J. L., Quiroz, J. A., Gould, T. D., Zarate, C. A., & Husseini, K. M. (2004). The cellular neurobiology of bipolar disorder. In D. S. Charney & E. J. Nestler (Eds.), *Neurobiology of Mental Illness*, Second Edition (pp. 397–420). New York: Oxford.

Powley, T. L., & Phillips, R. J. (2004). Gastric satiation is volumetric, intestinal satiation is nutritive. *Physiology and Behavior 82*: 69–74.

Raisman, G., & Field, P. (1971). Sexual dimorphism in the preoptic area of the rat. *Science 173*: 731–733.

Ratti, E., & Trist, D. (2001). Continuing evolution of the drug discovery process in the pharmaceutical industry. *Pure and Applied Chemistry 73*: 67–75.

Ritter, R. C. (2004). Gastrointestinal mechanisms of satiation for food. *Physiology and Behavior 81*: 249–273.

Robinson, L. A., Berman, J. S., & Neimeyer, R. A. (1990). Psychotherapy for the treatment of depression: A comprehensive review of controlled outcome research. *Psychological Bulletin 108*: 30–49.

Rocha, B. A., Scearce-Levie, K., Lucas, J. J., Hiroi, N., Castanon, N., Crabbe, J. C., Nestler, E. J., & Hen, R. (1998). Increased vulnerability to cocaine in mice lacking the serotonin-1B receptor. *Nature 393*: 175–178.

Romano, S. J., Halmi, K. A., Sarkar, N. P., Koke, S. C., & Lee, J. S. (2002). A placebo-controlled study of fluoxetine in continued treatment of bulimia nervosa after successful acute fluoxetine treatment. *American Journal of Psychiatry 159*: 96–102.

Roy-Byrne, P. P., & Cowley, D. S. (2002). Pharmacological treatments for panic disorder, generalized anxiety disorder, specific phobia, and social anxiety. In P. E. Nathan & J. M. Gorman (Eds.), *A Guide to Treatments That Work*, Second Edition (pp. 337–365). New York: Oxford.

Russell, R. W. (1987). Drugs as tools for research in neuropsychobiology: A historical perspective. *Neuropsychobiology 18*: 134–143.

Schlaug, G., Jancke, L., Huang, Y. & Steinmetz, H. (1995). In vivo evidence of structural brain asymmetry in musicians. *Science 267*: 699–701.

Schwartz, M. W. (2001). Brain pathways controlling food intake and body weight. *Experimental Biology and Medicine 226*: 978–981.

Schwartz, M. W., Woods, S. C., Seeley, R. J., Barsh, G. S., Baskiin, D. G., & Leibel, R. L. (2003). Is the energy homeostasis system inherently biased toward weight gain? *Diabetes 52*: 232–238.

Seibyl, J. P., Scanley, B. E., Krystal, J. H., & Innis, R. B. (2004). Neuroimaging methodologies: Utilizing radiotracers or nuclear magnetic resonance. In D. S. Charney & E. J. Nestler (Eds.), *Neurobiology of Mental Illness*, Second Edition (pp. 190–209). New York: Oxford.

Self, D. W., Barnhart, W. J., Lehman, D. A. & Nestler, E. J. (1996). Opposite modulation of cocaine-seeking behavior by D1- and D2-like dopamine receptor agonists. *Science 271*: 1586–1589.

Simerly, R. B., Swanson, L. W., & Gorski, R. A. (1984). Demonstration of a sexual dimorphism in the distribution of serotonin-immunoreactive fibers in the medial preoptic nucleus of the rat. *The Journal of Comparative Neurology 225*: 151–166.

Singer, J. (1968). Hypothalamic control of male and female sexual behavior in female rats. *Journal of Comparative and Physiological Psychology 66*: 738–742.

Smith, G. P. (1995). Dopamine and food reward. *Progress in Psychobiology and Physiological Psychology 16*: 83–144.

Smith, G. P., & Gibbs, J. (1994). Satiating effect of cholecystokinin. *Annals of the New York Academy of Sciences 713*: 236–241.

Sporn, J., Belanoff, J. K., Schatzberg, A. & Charney, D. S. (2004). Principles of the pharmacotherapy of depression. In D. S. Charney & E. J. Nestler (Eds.), *Neurobiology of Mental Illness*, Second Edition (pp. 491–511). New York: Oxford.

Staley, J. K., Krishnan-Sarin, S., Zoghbi, S., Tamagnan, G., Fujita, M., Seibyl, J. P., Maciejewski, P. K., O'Malley, S., & Innis, R. B. (2001). Sex differences in [123I] beta-CIT SPECT measures of dopamine and serotonin transporter availability in healthy smokers and nonsmokers. *Synapse 15*: 275–284.

References

Stein, M. B., & Bienvenu, O. J. (2004). Diagnostic classification of anxiety disorders: DSM-V and beyond. In D. S. Charney & E. J. Nestler (Eds.), *Neurobiology of Mental Illness*, Second Edition (pp. 525–534). New York: Oxford.

Stellar, E. (1954). The physiology of motivation. *Psychological Review 61*: 5–22.

Stitzer, M. L., & Walsh, S. L. (1997). Psychostimulant abuse: The case for combined behavioral and pharmacological treatments. *Pharmacology Biochemistry and Behavior 57*: 457–470.

Swedo, S. E., & Snider, L. A. (2004). The neurobiology and treatment of obsessive-compulsive disorder. In D. S. Charney & E. J. Nestler (Eds.), *Neurobiology of Mental Illness*, Second Edition (pp. 628–638). New York: Oxford.

Tamminga, C. A. (2004). Principles of the pharmacotherapy of schizophrenia. In D. S. Charney & E. J. Nestler (Eds.), *Neurobiology of Mental Illness*, Second Edition (pp. 339–354). New York: Oxford.

Tanda, G., Pontieri, F. E., & Di Chiara, G. (1997). Cannabinoid and heroin activation of mesolimbic dopamine transmission by a common mu opioid receptor mechanism. *Science 276*: 2048–2050.

Teitelbaum, P., & Epstein, A. N. (1962). The lateral hypothalamic syndrome: Recovery of feeding and drinking after lateral hypothalamic damage. *Psychological Review 69*: 74–90.

Teneud, L. M., Baptista, T., Murzi, E., Hoebel, B. G., & Hernandez, L. (1996). Systemic and local cocaine increase extracellular serotonin in the nucleus accumbens. *Pharmacology Biochemistry and Behavior 53*: 747–752.

Volkow, N. D., Chang, L., Wang, G.-J., Fowler, J. S., Dding, Y.-S., Sedler, M., Logan, J., Franceschi, D., Gatley, J., Hitzemann, R., Gifford, A., Wong, C., & Pappas, N. (2001). Low level of brain dopamine D2 receptors in methamphetamine abusers: Association with metabolism in the orbitofrontal cortex. *American Journal of Psychiatry 158*: 2015–2021.

Volkow, N. D., Fowler, J. S., Wolf, A. P., Schlyer, D., Shiuee, C. Y., Albert, R. (1990). Effects of chronic cocaine abuse on postsynaptic dopamine receptors. *American Journal of Psychiatry 147*: 719–724.

Volkow, N. D., Wang, G.-J., Fowler, J. S., Logan, J., Gatley, S. J., Gifford, A., Hitzemann, R., Ding, Y.-S., & Pappas, N. (1999). Prediction of reinforcing responses to psychostimulants in humans by brain dopamine D2 receptor levels. *American Journal of Psychiatry 156*: 1440–1443.

Volkow, N. D., Wang, G.-J., Fowler, J. S., Logan, J., Gatley, S. J., Hitzemann, R., Chen, A. D., & Pappas, N. (1997). Decreased striatal dopaminergic responsiveness in detoxified cocaine-dependent subjects. *Nature 386*: 830–833.

Wang, G.-J., Volkow, N. D., Logan, J., Pappas, N. R., Wong, C. T., Zhu, W., Netusil, N., & Fowler, J. S. (2001). Brain dopamine and obesity. *Lancet 3*: 354–357.

Wilson, G. T., & Fairburn, C. G. (2002). Treatments for eating disorders. In P. E. Nathan & J. M. Gorman (Eds.), *A Guide to Treatments That Work*, Second Edition (pp. 559–592). New York: Oxford.

Wise, R. A. (1997). Drug self-administration viewed as ingestive behavior. *Appetite 28*: 1–5.

Wong, D. F., Wagner, H. N., Tune, L. E., Dannals, R. F., Pearlson, G. D., Links, J. M., Tamminga, C. A., Broussolle, E. P., Ravert, H. T., Wilson, A. A., Toung, J. K. T., Malat, J., Williams, J. A., O'Tuama, L. A., Snyder, S. H., Kuhar, M. J., & Gjedde, A. (1986). Positron emission tomography reveals elevated D2 dopamine receptors in drug-naïve schizophrenics. *Science 234*: 1558–1563.

Woods, S. C. (2004). Lessons in the interactions of hormones and ingestive behavior. *Physiology and Behavior 82*: 187–190.

Woods, S. C., Seeley, R. J., Porte D., Jr., & Schwartz, M. W. (1998). Signals that regulate food intake and energy homeostasis. *Science 280*: 1378–1383.

Yehuda, R., Marshall, R., Penkower, A. & Wong, C. M. (2002). Pharmacological treatments for posttraumatic stress disorder. In P. E. Nathan & J. M. Gorman (Eds.), *A Guide to Treatments That Work*, Second Edition (pp. 411–445). New York: Oxford.

Yonkers, K. A., Kando, J. C., Cole, J. O., & Blumenthal, S. (1992). Gender differences in pharmacokinetics and pharmacodynamics of psychotropic medication. *American Journal of Psychiatry 149*: 587–595.

Index

Index

DATE DUE

17 yrs	